EASY LIFELONG
GARDENING

EASY LIFELONG
GARDENING

A PRACTICAL GUIDE FOR SENIORS

JOHN PIERCE

ROLAND BARNSLEY

Trafalgar Square Publishing

NORTH POMFRET, VERMONT

ISBN 0-943955-72-6

First published in the United States of America in 1993
by Trafalgar Square Publishing, North Pomfret, Vermont 05053.

Originally published in Canada by Key Porter Books Limited,
Toronto, Ontario, Canada.

Illustrations by Malcolm Cullen
Typesetting: MacTrix DTP
Printed and bound in Canada

93 94 95 96 97 6 5 4 3 2 1

Dedicated to the spirit of gardening,
and all who share its joys.

CONTENTS

PREFACE

This book is for all kinds of gardeners, senior or otherwise, whether handicapped, atrophied of limb or mind, or just a bit lazy. It's also for those of sound mind and body who want to make gardening easier, in order to allow time for life's other rewarding activities. We think you'll discover here a host of new tools, gardening equipment and ideas, and practical things you can do to extend your gardening years throughout your lifetime.

Whatever your physical condition, we have suggestions that will make your gardening chores easier. Both authors are seniors, and we have been experiencing physical limitations that prompted us to look for ways we could continue gardening well into the future. One of the things we discovered was a design science called ergonomics, which over the past decade has been used in industry to change tools and workplaces to fit the user. The idea of adapting products and workplaces to the user is becoming a consideration in the field of gardening. And the study of body movements, kinesiology, is contributing a better understanding of how to move properly, in order to avoid body strain when gardening. Both of these sciences are doing a lot to make gardening less physically wearing.

Although we present this book as a garden information source for the amateur senior gardener, it will also be useful for the professional garden designer who is serving seniors. We realize that gardening professionals are all busy trying to make a living, and don't have as much time as they would like in which to keep up with new developments. Since we are retired, we have the time to collect current gardening literature, to belong to the appropriate organizations, to attend seminars and conferences around the world, and to keep track of new state-of-the-art advancements.

Much has changed in gardening during our lifetime, since our apprenticeships date back to an era when fertilizer was barnyard manure and wheelbarrows had wooden tires. One thing that hasn't changed is the popularity of gardening! According to the National Gardening Association, which conducts an annual poll of America's favorite outdoor leisure activities, active gardening is enjoyed by more people than is cycling, fishing, jogging, tennis, or golf.

Our suggestions for making gardening easier are all based on personal know-how. Together we have had more than one hundred years of gardening experience — in teaching, in the practical fields of landscape design and construction, and in solving problems, whether for a developer with a one-thousand-acre landscaping project or for the disabled urban homeowner with a small back garden. We have traveled over much of the planet on work and study missions related

to horticulture and gardening, from San Diego to Tajikistan, from the Amazon to Hudson Bay, in search of the
old and the new in garden practice. We hope that our
experience will help you to pursue many years of gardening pleasure.

ACKNOWLEDGMENTS

Many people are involved in getting a book into print and we are fortunate to have a very competent publisher and a host of friends. For expert advice we want to thank Dr. J.P. MacMillan and Dr. Stuart McGill. For professional input, thanks to Dr. Henry M. Cathey, Dr. Diane Relf, Dr. Hugh Knowles, Brian Holley, and Sally Williams. For perceptive reading, our gratitude to Herschel Swanson. For very thorough, thoughtful editing, we were fortunate to have Wendy Thomas. For contributing in various ways that made the book possible: Lou Lafortune, Jim Cunning, Dorothea Schaab, Evelyn Salamanowicz, and Marian Swanson Pierce.

INTRODUCTION

With the growing concern for our planet and the threat posed by excessive consumerism, major changes are reshaping the way we live and the way we garden. People are looking toward adopting a simpler and healthier life-style. Whether you are a senior whose physical condition is beginning to limit your activities, or someone who wants to pare down your gardening chores, this book will show you how to manage your garden and make gardening a more relaxing and enjoyable pastime.

Unlike the hippie generation that just followed the flowers, most of us are firmly rooted in urban or suburban living. Like old trees, a major uprooting at maturity, such as moving into a nursing home, can be very traumatic, if not fatal. Gardening in very limited circumstances is still possible, however, as we will demonstrate.

Most garden books treat design entirely from the standpoint of how the garden looks, making the garden the focus. Our approach is to make the person the focus and design the garden to fit the gardener.

Whether you are a landscape architect or a home owner, you will find here practical ways to apply ergonomics and kinesiology to gardening. We present information and advice that will familiarize the limited-ability gardener with new, ergonomically designed tools and equipment that make gardening easier.

GARDENING INFORMATION

There is a great difference between garden writers and professional horticulturists who write about gardens. We would like to suggest that you give some thought to the quality of gardening information that you absorb. There are garden columns in the weekend papers, but we find that these have both advantages and disadvantages. Some of them are written by journalists who mean well, but don't have the background to properly restate what an expert has told them. It is a good idea to check to see which columnists have practical horticultural training and experience, and use them for your information sources.

The average North American can get a good deal of garden information from the weekend garden shows on television and radio. If you want to see gardens all over North America without doing any traveling, then tune in to these programs. With your VCR you can watch any of the new videos that are appearing every week, which seem to cover every aspect of gardening. In addition, you can get involved in activities such as the Master Gardener Program, workshops and courses at botanical gardens and arboreta, and seminars conducted by plant societies and garden clubs. You might be surprised by the scope of the garden information provided by botanical gardens and arboreta all over North America and Britain. For example, the Royal

Botanical Gardens in Hamilton, Ontario, lists more than 50 courses and workshops in gardening conducted by professional horticulturists, and the same happens at many places in North America. There are more than 400 botanical gardens and arboreta in North America, and these institutions all publish journals or information brochures on many aspects of gardening.

In Britain, the Horticultural Trades Association publishes one of the best full-color books of garden plants that we have seen, and similar information pamphlets are put out by the Landscape Trades Association in Canada and the American Nurseryman's Association in the United States. Your aim should be quality of information, so select your sources carefully.

In April 1992 we attended the second annual People-Plant Council Symposium at Rutgers University in New Jersey. The council is a clearing house for information and research results that cover all aspects of the interaction between people and plants, including gardening. The council is currently compiling a bibliographic data base — to date, it contains over 2000 listings. It is available on disk or as a printed list of 450 pages. This is a good source of information for landscape architects, horticultural therapists, and even individuals doing their own designs. The results of the first symposium held in 1991 are available in a book by Diane Relf (88)* that will give you an idea of the broad scope of the People-Plant Council.

* These numbers will help you find the specific source listed in the Sources section at the end of the book.

OUR ATTITUDES TOWARD PLANTS

Most gardeners are plant lovers, but the general population knows very little about them. They don't realize that their very lives depend upon plants, nor have they discovered the pleasures of gardening. You can help improve the attitudes of the public toward plants. Give someone a tree as a birthday present and be there to help plant it.

The public's ignorance is reflected in the way plants are ignored. We could tell many stories of having to fight to save an urban woodland in cities where urban forests are rapidly being replaced by housing and industry. Attitudes are changing, but not as fast as our culture.

Some environmental designers and planners have virtually ignored plants and made no serious provision for using them in urban planning. Many political meetings are preoccupied with zoning changes, severance of land and tax base assessments, with no room on the agenda for positive environmental planning. Perhaps achieving a clean, green environment cannot solve all of today's social and economic problems, but it can give us a sense of pride in being a part of nature, instead of succumbing to the vanity of being nature's overlord.

Planners need to realize that large trees and quantities of plants enhance the environment because of the functions they perform, and that we should preserve and protect public and private urban forested areas while we can. Once an urban woodland is gone, it cannot be replaced for any amount of money, and yet in many cities trees are being cut down for buildings faster than the park departments can plant new ones.

As the landscape that surrounds us becomes more man-made, plants and especially trees are a reminder that we are a part of nature rather than separate from it. If your property is full of plants, then you are doing your part to keep both yourself and your environment in good health. You can talk to and write to appropriate officials at all levels of government to urge them to use plants to improve your city, province or state, and country.

Here is some ammunition to use in your talks and letters! What do plants do for our environment that money cannot do?

PLANTS:
- are air conditioners, controlling temperature in the urban desert and providing shade protection from solar radiation.
- scrub dust and particulate matter out of the air.
- absorb sound and reduce excessive noise.
- breathe in pollutants and exhale oxygen.
- turn barren vacant lots into parks for people.
- screen the ugliness that man creates.
- provide privacy and define spaces.
- control soil erosion and maintain soil–water balance.
- enhance our quality of life and foster physical, mental, and spiritual well-being.
- provide the food and medicine that permit us to stay alive on this planet.

- contribute, with landscapes, to our personal and community sense of pride.

Authorities underestimate plants when they use them for beautification only; when they forget that without plants we couldn't survive on Earth; when they neglect their value in solving our environmental problems; and when they ignore their capacity to keep us healthy and able to enjoy our gardening.

Just recently there has been renewed interest in the Neem Tree (*Melia azedarach*), which contains chemicals that can control up to 200 insect pests without harming birds and bees. Medicinally, the tree compounds kill some bacteria; control malaria; show promise of blocking fertility in both men and women; and are a source of soap, oils, and lubricants. The Neem Tree was listed in Sanskrit medical literature 1000 years ago, but we are slow to learn! How many other such trees are we losing because we disregard plants?

We gardeners need to widen the public's attitude toward plants to include their value for architectural uses, engineering and climate control, fostering good health, and formulating chemical compounds for man, in addition to their current use in beautification programs and in recreation. Everyone forgets that we are guests of the plants on this planet!

PART ONE

NEW INSIGHTS FOR ALL SENIOR GARDENERS

AT ABOUT RETIREMENT AGE, MANY OF US DEVELOP SOME physical infirmities. This book will show that you don't have to abandon gardening when faced with the problems of aging. An understanding of body movement is the first step in the preparation of a new approach to the physical side of gardening.

New discoveries in kinesiology, the study of body movement, are turning up ways to make gardening easier for all age groups, and especially for those of us who have limited physical abilities. As the body ages, it has less elasticity and flexibility. Understanding kinesiology can help keep you healthy.

We tend to think of the aging human body as a machine that wears out from constant use, but actually the body stays in better condition, and ages more slowly, with exercise like gardening. When you begin to say, "Oh! I can't do *that* any more!" you send a message to your brain that you are giving up. If you keep trying to do things, the message to the brain is "Repair the parts!"

In children we find an instinctive pattern of constant motion, called kinesophilia, which insures that the young developing body gets the proper exercise. During the aging process, this pattern diminishes, so aging well means exercising the body and the mind — and gardening does both!

CHAPTER 1

BODY MOVEMENT AND BODY CARE

THE GOAL OF LIFE IS TO DIE YOUNG — AS LATE AS POSSIBLE!
— *Ashley Montagu*

BODY MOVEMENT

Many universities in North America are doing research that involves understanding and improving the techniques of body movement. We visited one of these research facilities at the University of Waterloo in Ontario, where Dr. Stuart McGill took us through the Occupational Biomechanics Laboratories in the Department of Kinesiology. Here they conduct all kinds of tests to improve the way people use the body in the workplace, and many of their results also apply to the activities involved in gardening.

Studies of lifting, testing of insoles in shoes to determine the capacity of the foam to dissipate energy, and using a vibrating chair to find the effect of vibration on the spine are samples of the type of work being done in university laboratories. A gardening example consists of tests to determine how much strain using a bent shovel puts on the back! Normally a shovelful of soil is pitched off to the side, creating a force on the body that can result in back strain, so unfortunately the modified shovel design doesn't solve this problem.

The body movements of gardening are similar to those of the workplace, and learning to make these movements properly can help you keep your body in tip-top condition. Using ergonomic tools and equipment, such as those discussed in Chapter 2, will help you make the correct body movements.

Here are some suggestions for the proper body movements and the type of equipment to use when performing common gardening tasks:

Raking

For most of us, the main purpose of raking is getting leaves into a container to put on the compost pile or into flower beds for mulch. We both use bamboo leaf rakes because they are so light. When you shop for a leaf rake, you'll find them made of light metal like aluminum, various kinds of light plastic, and heavier steel. To conserve your energy, get a light leaf rake.

When using a leaf rake, keep the rake handle within a few inches of your body and use short strokes, not reaching out too far. When you keep your elbows close to your body you are using more muscles, and raking is easier than with your arms extended. Using the appropriate ergonomic tools, described in Chapter 2, you can perhaps eliminate the need for raking leaves.

Digging

A shovel with a keen, sharp edge will go into the ground more easily than a dull one. Use either a coarse file or a sharpener that fits an electric drill in order to keep a sharp edge on your shovel. Again, keep the shovel close to your body, and when you push the shovel down into the earth with your right foot, lean forward a bit and slightly bend your left leg. In Chapter 2, several ergonomic tools that are easier to use for loosening the soil than the standard shovel are described.

Shoveling
Let's say you are shoveling compost for your flower beds into a wheelbarrow. If the compost is light, use a standard-sized shovel that is spoon-shaped with a pointed tip, and when you lift the shovelful keep your elbows in close to your body to get better leverage. Move your body close to the wheelbarrow and turn the shovel upside down to empty it. The handle of the shovel should be at least 4 feet (1.2 m) long. For this kind of work you can get a very light aluminum shovel that is easy to handle.

Weeding
You can greatly reduce or eliminate weeding by using some of the ergonomic equipment described in Chapter 2, such as a permanent mulch weed-control mat. If you plan to weed with a hoe, try a sharp scuffle hoe that glides through the soil with a to-and-fro motion that is much easier on your back than the chopping motion of a regular hoe. Some people prefer a light weed hook that has a small blade sharpened on both edges for push-and-pull cutting just below the

soil surface, and long-handled weed pullers are available for people who should avoid bending, or for use from a wheelchair (28).*

There are many different types of hoes, and you may want to test out several types to find the one you like best. A good way to do this is to join a garden club, talk to the members, and get them to let you try the tools they are using. Most gardeners love to show off their favorite tools.

You should avoid long periods of work in a position where your trunk is flexed forward. This position stretches passive tissues in your back, which require time to return to their original shape once you resume an upright stance. After long periods of bending, return to a vertical position for several minutes before doing more work.

Ergonomic equipment design will now let you sit and weed raised beds, or kneel on soft pads to plant spring bulbs, and at the same time minimize the pull of gravity on your body. Gardening this way helps the body expand to a full range of movement and releases tension stored in the muscles.

Pruning

The important thing in pruning is to keep the wrist straight. Unfortunately, the average pair of hand pruners bends the wrist into an unnatural position that

---

* These numbers will help you find the specific source listed in the Sources section at the end of the book.

causes static muscular strain. You should buy hand pruners with the cutting blades offset at an angle that avoids this problem, or perhaps try a ratchet hand pruner. The ratchet pruner cuts into the wood only a quarter of an inch (6 mm) every time you squeeze with little hand pressure. Several light squeezes will cut easily through a thick branch. For many pruning jobs, a light pair of long-handled ratchet loppers requires less effort than hand pruners.

For larger limbs, you can't beat a small folding pruning saw that cuts on the pull stroke. Sawing on the pull stroke means less binding and bending than with a carpenter's saw that cuts on the push stroke. You can cut a 3-inch (7.5-cm) branch in seconds! It is probably best to call a professional tree care company for large-tree pruning.

For long hedges, an electric pruner is the tool to use. To reduce the need for pruning, you can root prune a hedge, and perhaps top prune only every other year. The movement you want to avoid in pruning is tipping the head back when trying to reach high overhead. (You should be careful when hanging out clothes, since this involves a very similar movement.) You can get a very sturdy short ladder that will raise you, so that you don't have the strain of reaching. If you have a balance problem, let someone help you.

Root Pruning
Root pruning is one of the garden practices that we often overlook, but it is a good way to slow down plant

growth. The ultimate root-pruning exercise is bonsai, where trimming roots and top at the same time slows the growth so much that some 400-year-old cedar trees are only 4 feet (1.2 m) high.

To root prune a hedge, use a razor-sharp spade with a blade about a foot (30.5 cm) long. Press the spade as far into the ground as it will go, approximately a foot (30.5 cm) from the main stem. Follow this procedure along the length of the hedge on both sides. This cuts off some of the young feeder roots and so slows the growth of the top. You can prune along the same line in successive years. We have both used this practice on hedges and trees to reduce the need for top pruning.

Cultivating

For loosening garden soil without a lot of bending, there are several types of wheel cultivators that require short pushing-and-pulling motions, but no bending of the back. We usually use the high wheel model, which goes over the ground smoothly and easily. These tools are available with cultivator teeth or scuffle-hoe blades for weeding while you cultivate.

If your condition permits, you can reduce weeding time by using a lightweight gasoline or electric cultivator. Some models weigh only 20 pounds (9 kg) and are easy to handle.

Planting

You can dig the holes for bulbs and other small plants with long-handled tools, which require very little bending. However, you almost have to get down on a kneeling pad or individual knee pads to do your planting properly, and there are several different kinds of ergonomic devices described in Chapter 2 to help you do this.

If you are down on your hands and knees for a fairly long period, try flexing your abdominal muscles by pulling your stomach in, for a change of muscle tensions.

Mowing
As you age, sometimes the simplest solution to the mowing problem is to cut down the size of your lawn by paving or planting ground cover. But it is certainly possible to find the right mowing equipment for your physical ability.

Many seniors will find that the new lightweight hand mowers give them just the right amount of exercise when cutting a small lawn. For active older gardeners who have bigger lawns, there are riding mowers and self-propelled walking mowers.

We have a friend who uses a hand mower because he enjoys the rhythmic click-click of the whirling blades as they cut. We are both old enough to recall the sweeping swish of a scythe as it slices through the grass.

You can now use a much-improved and comfortable electric mower with no cord to drag around, described in Chapter 2. The electric car is barely off the drawing board, but we bet you'll soon find cordless electric mowers in every hardware store.

Watering

If you use a hose nozzle to do your watering, use a pistol-grip nozzle to keep your wrist straight. It is important to remember that when you are screwing and unscrewing nozzles or jars, you should keep your elbows up against your body for maximum muscle strength. Don't reach and twist!

When you stretch your arm out straight to perform a twisting motion, you are using only the

Instead of using only the muscles of the forearm when you twist (A), keep your elbow close to your body so that you use the muscles both in the forearm and the upper arm (B).

muscles of the forearm. If you pull your elbow in close to your body and do the same twisting motion, you are using both the muscles in the forearm and the biceps in the upper arm, which gives you greater strength.

Moving Garden Freight

There is now a motorized wheelbarrow on the market for the active senior gardener, but you still have to load it with what you want to move. For most of us, a better vehicle for moving large loads of garden material is the big-wheel garden cart. It is not motorized, but is balanced so that it moves easily and unloads by tipping forward.

If your property is large enough to warrant it, you can get an electric, flatbed vehicle like the ones used in many nurseries for moving plants.

There are about 20 different brands of big-wheel garden carts. Select one that has pneumatic tires and a dump front for easy loading and unloading without lifting. Such a cart will move up to 300 pounds (136 kg) of compost very easily.

Lifting
1. Wear a high-bib apron so you can bring the object up against your chest.
2. Keep your back straight — DO NOT bend at the waist.
3. Bend your knees and squat.
4. Tense the abdominal muscles and lift with the big muscles of your legs, keeping your back straight.

Proper movements for lifting include keeping your back straight and bending your legs.

Carrying

Somewhere back in time, Orientals discovered that the easiest way to lift and carry was to use a shoulder yoke that evenly distributed the weight to both sides of the body. In Burma even today, you don't have to go far to see men and women with watering cans hanging from both ends of a yoke. They go to the lake and fill the cans while they are still attached to the yoke, so that the lifting is done with the whole body, not just the arms. When they get to a flower bed, they simply tip the cans, exerting very little strain on the wrists or elbows. If you want to experiment with using a yoke and surprise your neighbors, there may be one available at The Marugg Co., Tracy City, Tennessee 37387.

AVOIDING STRAIN

The body is a muscle machine, and there are some positions and postures that create more strain than others. Here are some guidelines for cutting down on strain:

1. **Avoid reaching and twisting**. Keep whatever you're working on right in front of you, and rather than twisting around to get a pair of pruners, turn your whole body. Instead of reaching with your arms to pick something up, move your whole body closer to the object.
2. **Bending**. When you are bending over to pick something up, bend your knees slightly and let your thighs carry the weight of your body and the object you are retrieving. The upper body weighs about 80–90 pounds (36–40 kg), so every time you bend over and then lift the weight of your upper body, you are using unnecessary energy and putting stress on the spine. Whenever you are picking up heavy objects, you should squat instead of bending over.
3. **Sitting**. Avoid the pull of gravity by sitting on the ground, on the edge of a raised bed, or on one of the new ergonomic stools. Most Westerners find it difficult to sit on their heels, but Asians do much of

their work in this position. When John was visiting a
family in Yokosuka, Japan, they took him on a train
trip to Atami to visit relatives of theirs who had
chairs. After watching him try to sit on his heels,
they had thought that Westerners needed chairs!

4. **On hands and knees.** We have both had the experience of trying to stand up after a long session on the
hands and knees planting bulbs, only to find that the
sacroiliac joint (where the pelvis and the backbone are
joined) was out and the pain was intense. Sitting on
our heels is uncomfortable, but we find the ergonomic
stool a good way to work at lower levels without
twisting or straining the trunk. (See Chapter 2.)

These suggestions should help you to learn to
move your body properly, so that you can avoid injury
and look forward to many more years of happy gardening. Industrial ergonomics has been an active field
for about the last 10 years, and places such as the
School of Human Biology at the University of Guelph
in Ontario, and many others, have greatly reduced
workplace injuries resulting from faulty body movement and other factors such as poor lighting.

In Chapter 2, you will find a discussion of
ergonomic tools that are available to make your gardening activities easier. If you would like more information about body movements, we would suggest that
you find the nearest university doing this type of
research and pay it a visit.

BODY CARE
Body Conditioning
There are several schools of body exercise and treatment designed to improve the mobility of the aging body, but most active older gardeners don't need them. If you have been gardening for several years, then your body is probably in pretty good condition. As physical limitations increase, however, it is worth learning to use the body wisely.

We find that swimming is one of the best ways to keep the body flexible and functioning smoothly. Perhaps you should consider adding a swim spa to your home property. If there isn't room, then you might want to add a lean-to greenhouse to have more space for plants and also accommodate your spa.

Warm Up
Before you go out to the garden, try the following preparatory movements suggested by the American Physical Therapy Association.

1. Slowly move your head from side to side.
2. Slowly raise each knee as high as possible above the waist.
3. With feet apart and hands on hips, gently rotate the upper body.
4. Clench hands tightly and release.
5. Rotate wrists in circles.

These are really movements, rather than exercises, and they suggest other long-established movement activities such as T'ai Chi and Feldenkreis. When Moshe Feldenkreis lost the use of his knees after a soccer injury, he developed a set of movements to restore the use of his knees. Most of the movements are done slowly, lying down or sitting to reduce the pull of gravity on the body (13).

The proper or optimum amount of exercise for older people varies with the individual, and each of us must determine this for himself or herself. Mind over matter *does* work, and if you have stiff joints in the morning, mild exercise such as gardening may well loosen up all the body joints and make you more comfortable.

USING PLANTS FOR BODY CARE
Cosmetics

You can grow many plants for both cosmetic and medicinal body care right in your own garden, and more gardeners are doing it every day! As we age, perhaps the most noticeable change is in the condition of the skin. In your home garden or greenhouse, you can grow roses, strawberries, watercress, cucumbers, pears, and apricots, all of which contain skin treatment compounds. John's grandmother had a screen planting of elderberry in her backyard, and used the flowers for a facial herb steaming treatment. Many women grow their own plants to have fresh ingredients for bath oils, soaps, and lotions.

Medicines

Imagine a Neanderthal woman with a rash on her arm, reaching for a plant leaf to rub on it. Discovering that the rash healed quickly, she applied the same plant leaf to other skin problems, and the use of plants for body care began.

Since that time, we have seen the African witch doctor, the Asian shaman, the North American medicine man, and the Chinese herbalist all using plants in their therapy rituals. Long before man or drugstores, plants were formulating alkaloids, and physicians still use many natural plant alkaloids, as well as synthetic ones. Among these are the vitamins that play a major role in body care.

Vitamins

We are all aware that vitamins are necessary for body health, but only recently have we discovered that they may also foster mental health. Some authors are even using the term "brain food" for certain vitamins.

Some people have the notion that you can get all the vitamins you need from a properly balanced diet. That may have been true when Grandmother grew her own food on the farm, but today we all eat food that is grown without regard for vitamin content. This suggests that growing your own vitamin plants in a garden or greenhouse is a good way to stay healthy. During the day, the plant manufactures vitamins, and at night uses them in the growth process. When you grow your own vitamin plants, you can pick them fresh, in the late afternoon when the vitamin content is high.

As the body ages, its production of vitamins declines, and the right amount of vitamin supplements may be beneficial. In the state of Washington, 65% of registered dietitians use vitamin supplements daily. Each of us is a unique physiological system, so remember that vitamins may have different effects on different people.

There is an increasing amount of writing in books and magazines about what different vitamins and minerals can do for human body functions. If you have experience in this field, you can research this literature and decide for yourself what vitamin supplements to take. Otherwise, we suggest that you let your doctor or nutritionist advise you.

Many vitamins are stored in the body:

Vitamin A: (Beta Carotene): Found in green and yellow vegetables such as spinach, broccoli, carrots, and sweet potatoes; in green and yellow fruits such as kiwi, avocado, squash, and cantaloupe.

Vitamin D: The raw materials to make vitamin D exist in plants. Animals and fish eat plants, and we eat fish oils, tuna, sardines, eggs, and milk to get our vitamin D. When you expose your skin to sunlight, the skin oils are converted to vitamin D, although a heavy suntan stops the process.

Vitamin E: Found in many foods, such as green vegetables, broccoli, brussels sprouts, wheat germ, spinach, whole grains, and vegetable oils.

Vitamin K: Found in alfalfa, sunflower, soya, tomatoes, orange peel, kelp, and liver.

Other vitamins are not stored in the body:

Vitamin B_1 (Thiamine): Found in nuts, whole grains, egg yolk, brewer's yeast, asparagus, peas, and beans.

Vitamin B_2 (Riboflavin): Found in spinach, organ meats, milk, brewer's yeast, and parsley.

Vitamin B_3 (Niacin): Found in nuts, whole grains, spinach, prunes, figs, tomato juice, avocado, and organ meats.

Vitamin B_5 (Pantothenic acid): Found in most vegetables, peas, whole grains, brewer's yeast, and organ meats.

Vitamin B_6 (Pyridoxine): Found in whole grain rice, cabbage, barley, corn, and beef liver.

Vitamin B_{12} (Cobalamin): Found only in animal tissue — meat, poultry, fish, and dairy products. Vegetarians beware! There is some in the herb *comfrey*, but you'd have to eat about 5 pounds (2.3 kg) to get enough.

Vitamin C (Ascorbic acid): Found in rose hips, citrus fruits, berries, green leafy vegetables, carrots, onions, tomatoes, peppers, and cantaloupe. Look into these for help with the common cold.

Biotin: Found in wheat germ, whole grain rice, and brewer's yeast.

Choline: Found in organ meats, wheat germ, egg yolk, and brewer's yeast.

ASK A THERAPIST

Talking with Maureen Phillips, a horticultural therapist master from Seattle, Washington, we discovered the kind of help that is available in services such as her "Design Consultation for the Elderly and Disabled." Her training permits her to assess physical conditions and design gardens to fit the needs of her clients. One of her specialities is designing a complete home/garden environment for wheelchair gardeners. If your present gardening activities are causing body problems, you might like to seek the services of a qualified therapist to suggest ways to make your gardening a pleasure again (5, 9, 17).

ASK YOUR DOCTOR

We were curious to know if a general practitioner had patients with problems related to gardening, so we went to talk with Dr. J.P. McMillan of Niagara-on-the-Lake, Ontario, who has a high percentage of older retired patients. He told us that in the spring, when the garden season starts, he usually has a sudden rush of patients with complaints about the back, head, and neck, from constantly getting up and down, pushing and reaching too high to do pruning. The new ergonomic tools are designed to help you avoid just such problems. He discovered that one patient had been down on her hands and knees for about three hours the day before, after a winter of relative in-activity. A sit stool or kneel stool would give her body a rest now and then.

Many older people have some arthritis in the hands and neck, which can affect circulation and cause muscle spasms in the neck. Arthritis has recently been showing up in younger age groups as well. If you exercise to keep the tone of the muscles good, you will have less trouble. Without exercise the muscles atrophy.

Stretch in bed in the morning before getting up, because the muscles have relaxed all night — even Olympic athletes do warm-up exercises. And remember when carrying things to have some weight on both sides for balance. When you carry a heavy weight on one side, it pulls the muscles on the other side and may cause strain. Dr. McMillan also recommends vitamins routinely for all his older patients because, as we age, the natural body production of vitamins declines.

Mental attitude is important — don't give up trying! Even the people who can't garden, for one reason or another, can profit by watching others, and then having something to talk or reminisce about. Horticultural therapy used to consist of bringing flowers to the sick, but it has come a long way. Gardening is a good therapy exercise, not competitive, but fulfilling and creative. It gives you a series of deadlines — a time to do this and a time to do that, and then sit back and enjoy the fruits of your labor. Gardening can also improve the quality of life, exercises the aesthetic senses, and is a pursuit open to almost anyone, no matter how disabled. Dr. McMillan has a patient who is 104 years old, and who still moves about her senior citizen's apartment with a walker, enjoying her houseplants!

Your doctor, like Dr. McMillan, probably treats older people with body complaints stemming from not moving properly. Ask your doctor for suggestions, like those mentioned above, about how to do your usual gardening chores properly, to avoid strain. If you have any physical problems that are causing discomfort, see a physician at once and perhaps have a therapist redesign your garden.

CHAPTER 2

EASY GARDENING TOOLS

TOOLS ARE AN EXTENSION OF MAN'S BRAIN AND
HANDS TO MAKE WORK EASIER.
— *Buckminster Fuller*

ERGONOMICS

Ergonomics is a type of biotechnology, applying knowledge about the mechanics of the human body to the design of tools and the environment, so that there is a comfortable fit between people, the things they use, and the places in which they work. Our aim is to help you create an ergonomic home landscape and garden to fit your physical condition, and we want to acquaint you with a variety of ergonomic tools that make gardening much easier for those of us with limited physical ability.

During World War II, engineers noticed that some aircraft cockpits were set up so that repetitions or tiring movements were required of the pilot. The engineers redesigned the cockpits to better fit the pilot. After the war, the word "ergonomics" was coined in Europe to designate this type of technology. An ergometer is a device for measuring the amount of work done, or the energy produced by a muscle or group of muscles.

Ergonomics has become a very active discipline, because of the physical problems that have developed

31

in various workplaces. People such as assembly line workers, grocery checkout clerks, and video display terminal operators can develop repetitive motion disorders such as carpal tunnel syndrome, a condition affecting the movement of the wrist. It takes the skills of an ergonomist to correct the causes of such problems.

Gardening often requires some of the particular motions that can cause physical problems. Fortunately, ergonomics is now changing gardening to create that better fit we spoke of earlier, between people, their gardens, and the tools they use. For example, an ergonomic trowel has been designed for people with arthritis in the fingers. This trowel uses the muscles of the palm of the hand for gripping, rather than the fingers. It is also designed to keep the wrist straight while digging.

We hear a lot about jogging, walking, and aerobic classes as exercise activities for seniors, and are apt to forget that gardening not only involves all the movements and exercise necessary to keep mobility at a good level, but at the same time fosters emotional health. Jogging or walking down the same route day after day can get to be a bore, but your garden changes with the seasons and keeps your interest high as you participate in the life process.

Every year new tools and equipment are designed and produced to make gardening easier, especially for those of us with limited physical ability. We describe below some of the most widely available ones, as well as some that may be hard to find. During the cold winter months study catalogs and magazines and discover what's new for you!

The number in parentheses at the end of each item refers to the Sources section at the end of the book, to tell you *one* of the places you can buy the product. Your local garden center may well stock these items, so ask there first!

RAKING

There are many kinds of rakes, each for a different purpose. To make gardening easy, you have to select the proper rake for the job. For raking stones and debris, and for leveling soil, you need a steel-tined rake with a flat head and a long handle. We like a German model, because it has a small "Helping Handle" that attaches to the long handle, in order to give you a firmer grip and better leverage when pulling the rake toward you. You can buy the "Helping Handle" grip separately and attach it to rakes you already own (50). A light aluminum rake from Denmark has low curved ends to get in under lower branches or to avoid the good plants in a row of vegetables.

Several brands of adjustable rakes are handy for tight spots. You can rake with the tines only 7 inches (18 cm) wide or, for leaves on the lawn, expand the tines to 23 inches (58 cm).

Roll-'n'-Rake: Some smart inventor has come up with a rake on wheels — no more stress and strain of cross-body pulling. It looks like a mower, but between the wheels is a rake that is adjustable for height (37).

Leaf Sweeper: The hand lawn sweeper has been around for a long time, and is still a good way to pick up leaves, wheel them to the compost, and dump them. This is one item that you'll find in almost every garden center or nursery.

Power Lawn Vacuum: There are several different brands of these devices that pick up leaves, using electric power. We like the electric models because they are quiet, are easy to operate and don't discharge pollutants into the air. One of these is a combination blower and vacuum shredder that you carry with a shoulder sling. It shreds the leaves as it picks them up, and reduces what might have been 10 bags of leaves to one. You can also use the blower to get leaves into the flower beds, where they will form an excellent mulch. Another blower that also mulches is on wheels, and has an ergonomically designed handle that keeps the wrist straight (48).

Grip-Sweep Rake: This lets you rake and then pick up leaves without bending over. It also converts into a broom (37).

Sweep Stick: This is a quiet, battery-powered blower that makes it easy to clean off patio and walks, or blow leaves off the lawn and into flower beds for mulch. A blower means that you don't have the problem of picking up leaves — you just move them around.

DIGGING
Trowel
The old-fashioned trowel is about to be replaced by a

new ergonomically designed tool made of very light and strong polycarbonate resin, which will not break, bend, or rust, and which feels warm to your hand. The handle is angled and shaped to fit into the palm of your hand. This design keeps your wrist straight and takes some of the strain off the muscles of the fingers, so that even with arthritis or carpal tunnel syndrome you can keep on using a trowel. The new type of handle makes the trowel easier to push into the soil; keep the edge sharp with an ordinary file. We should strike a medal

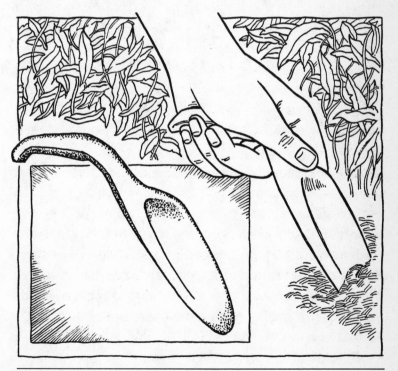

The new ergonomic trowel is designed so that the handle fits into the palm of your hand and keeps your wrist straight.

New equipment such as the Soil Digger makes loosening and aerating the soil much easier.

for the person who invented a tool to make it easier for older gardeners to keep on digging (38, 50)!

Ergonomic design now gives us long-handled hand hoes and trowels that are lightweight, but strong. The handles are long enough to be used when you are standing up. There are also tools that have wrist straps so that you won't drop them. You can use them either sitting down in a wheelchair or standing up, to easily extend your reach (28).

The Soil Digger is a new tool that was developed in

the Netherlands, where the soils are heavy, to make loosening and aerating an easier chore. Instead of trying to push a shovel blade into the ground, you step on a bar to push five round, steel tines into the soil with minimum effort. The tines are 11 inches (28 cm) long, and once they are in the ground, simply pull back to loosen the soil without doing any heavy lifting. This tool is certainly high on the list of aids that will make lifelong gardening easier (32).

WEEDING

If you enjoy using a hoe for weeding, we suggest a scuffle hoe that moves back and forth to cut the weeds without requiring you to lift the hoe or bend over. It comes with a 54-inch (137-cm) handle, so that you can easily reach all the weeds.

You can do your weeding from a wheelchair with a long-handled weed puller from England. It is designed to grip and pull tough weeds in cultivated ground, and can be operated with one hand (50). It doesn't work well in pulling tough weeds out of turf, so for this type of weeding we would recommend one of the long-handled tools that cuts rather than pulls lawn weeds (38).

MULCHING

If you would like to avoid weeding, try mulching with a new black paper mulch that allows water and air to get to the soil, and is 100% biodegradable. It comes in rolls 50 feet (15 m) long and 28 inches (71 cm) wide —

just the right size for raised beds. To plant, you simply cut a hole in the mulch and insert a plant. At the end of the season, you can till the mulch right into the soil.

PRUNING

A ratchet anvil pruner cuts a ¾-inch (19-mm) branch easily because when you squeeze the handle, the blade goes into the wood only about a quarter of an inch (6 mm) at a time. Squeeze again and it goes another quarter of an inch (6 mm), and so on until you have cut a thick branch and used only the muscle power needed for cutting a small branch.

The same type of cutting action is available in a pair of long-handled loppers for pruning branches over an inch (2.5 cm) thick. Once you try these, you'll never go back to pruners without the ratchet cutting action (50)!

Most pruning saws cut on the pull, rather than on the push-and-pull the way carpenters' saws do, and are much easier to use. One type is the Oregon saw, which has a unique tooth design that planes as it cuts to give you a nice smooth edge. We have often been at pruning parties where we would cut a branch and immediately have people come over to ask what kind of saw we were using, because we did it so easily and so fast. Many garden retailers now stock this type of pruner and we're sure you'll find one near you (40, 50). Also available is a new Japanese pruning saw with a 12-inch (30.5-cm) blade and a pistol-grip handle, which keeps the wrist in the proper position to avoid carpal tunnel syndrome (34).

We used to use tar products to coat the stub of a branch after pruning, but recent research has shown that the only material that promotes good callus formation, keeps the insects out, and lets the tissue breath is an organic, rubber-like spread called "Lac Balsam." In Europe it is called artificial bark because it is colored like bark (34).

CULTIVATING
By Hand
Of the many kinds of cultivators, the high-wheel type with the handles mounted over the axle is the easiest to move over the ground. The wheel is metal and about 2 feet (61 cm) in diameter (38). We like a model with inflated rubber tires and a swivel joint for the handles, so that you can walk in one row and cultivate or weed in the next. There are four attachments, including a scuffle hoe that is easy to use on a wheel device (32, 34). Healthy older gardeners like two handles for better balance and find that using this equipment gives them just about the right amount of exercise.

By Power
There are several makes of power tillers available, both gasoline and electric, and weighing about 20–25 pounds (9–11 kg). If you are comfortable with handling power equipment, these tillers do a fine job. We prefer the electric models because they are easier

to start and don't require gasoline that pollutes our air.

PLANTING
Planting Bar
New tools called planting bars are much easier for seniors to use than any type of shovel. The blade of the planting bar is 3 inches (7.5 cm) wide and 10 inches (25 cm) long. Such a narrow blade goes into the ground easily with slight foot pressure on the offset step. The T-handle is easy to grip and long enough to minimize bending over. You can use this tool for planting bedding plants, bulbs, and seedlings. Some of the nurseries plant thousands of tree seedlings every year and find this the best tool for the job (38, 50).

Seeding Tube
You can make a simple device for seeding without bending over. Get a 4-foot (1.2-m) piece of rigid PVC pipe at the hardware store and glue a small funnel in the top. Then place the tube exactly where you want it, and drop your seeds into the tube, without bending over.

Bulb Planter
To avoid too much work on your hands and knees when you are planting bulbs, use a long-handled bulb planter. The easiest method is to make all the holes for the bulbs and then use your knee pads to get down and plant them. This bulb planter will cut through sod easily if you want to plant daffodils in a lawn area (50).

Super Soft Kneeling Pad
This the best kneeling pad we've found. It is made of ¾-inch (1.8-cm) thick high density foam rubber and is inexpensive and widely available.

MAKE YOUR OWN SEEDLING POTS
An ingenious Canadian gardener has invented a little wooden molding device that lets you turn strips of newspaper into small pots without using any glue. You simply roll the newspaper on a wooden mold. Give it a little press into a wooden base and you have a dandy pot for seedlings that will decompose in the ground when you plant. Unless your hands are severely crippled, these pots are easy to make (34).

SOIL TESTING
For fifty cents per test you can make certain your soil is in optimum condition for growth with a new soil test kit called Rapitest, which measures pH as well as nitrogen, phosphorus, and potassium content. The kit is easier to use than some others on the market and contains everything you need to make about 60 tests (34).

HARVESTING
When it's time to pick some flowers for the house, there is no substitute for a long-handled cut-and-hold tool. The blades are stainless Sheffield steel and you can reach out almost 3 feet (91 cm) with a tool that weighs only 14 ounces (4 kg). This tool simplifies picking in raised beds and deep borders. It is just as good for

cutting flowers from climbers or hanging baskets (50).

When you want to pick fruit, use a long-handled fruit picker. Avoid reaching up and bending your head back. One model will reach 15 feet (4.5 m) high, and has a foam-lined wire basket in which to receive the fruit. Many of us find using this kind of equipment too strenuous, so we get a tall high school student to use it, and tell him what to pick.

GARDENING SITTING DOWN OR KNEELING
Single-Seat Kneeler

Once you have tried this 5-pound (2.3-kg) poly-ethylene stool, you'll never want to be without it. It will not rust, corrode, or dent. When it is upright, you sit on it; turn it upside down and you can kneel comfortably (40). There are also brands made of tubular steel, weighing about 10 pounds (4.5 kg).

Scoot'N Do

This cart is about 3 feet (91 cm) long and a foot (30.5 cm) wide, with a well-padded seat and large plastic wheels. You pull it around by a rope that is attached to its front. The Scoot'N Do has storage space for tools and seed packets, and will support up to 300 pounds (136 kg). One end has a shallow box that you can set pots in without having them fall off the edge. This is a good way to avoid strain on your back, knees, and legs.

Garden Scoot

The Garden Scoot is another way to garden sitting down — on a traditional old-fashioned tractor seat mounted on good wide rubber wheels that can easily navigate soft ground. The seat is on a pivot, so that it swivels around for easy work on either side or in any position (34).

Knee Pads

There are many manufacturers of knee pads, which are still a great convenience for getting down and into digging and planting. We like a pair that is easy to put on and take off, with Velcro straps that hold the knee pads in place (28). Again, it pays to look at several different makes before you buy.

When the Single-Seat Kneeler is upright, you can sit on it, and when it is upside down, you can kneel comfortably.

The Cane-Seat

If you enjoy walk-around gardening but like to stop once in a while for a rest, you should try a cane-seat. It is made of rigid aluminum and weighs only 2 pounds (1 kg). The seat folds up so that you can use it as a cane and then fold the seat down for a rest while you survey your handiwork. You'll find this convenient for field trips to nearby botanical gardens or visits to flower shows (34).

FEEDING

Slow-Release Tablets

You can reduce plant-feeding chores by using planting tablets that slowly release nitrogen, phosphorus, and potash constantly and steadily over a two- to three-year period. Most fertilizers are soluble in water and dissolve rather rapidly, but the good in planting tablets is not water soluble. The roots of your plants grow to the tablet and make contact with the fertilizer. To accomplish this, you punch holes into the root zone of your plants with a planting bar, and then drop the slow-release tablets into the holes. You have to attend to feeding only every second year.

Hose-end Devices

Another easy feeding method is to attach a jar containing soluble fertilizer to your hose and feed as you water. Several types are widely available. There is also a metering device that you can attach to your faucet,

This portable garden seat folds up so that it can also be used as a cane.

which lets you water and feed through a sprinkler or drip irrigation at the other end of the hose (38).

Root Feeders
An easy-to-use root feeder consists of a jar of soluble fertilizer with a long probe that you insert into the ground to put the fertilizer right into the root zone of the plants. The water pressure in the probe makes it go into the ground so easily that you could even use it from a wheelchair (38).

WATERING
Self-Watering Pots

If you plan to be away for some time, several brands of pots have a water reservoir in their base that allows capillary action to take the water up through a wick to the plant roots, over an extended period (50). Alternatively, you can make your own wick-watering containers that provide water as the plant needs it. Easy-watering pots come in all sizes, including a planter box about 16 inches (40.5 cm) long, which can be mounted on a shelf or even a wide window sill (31, 32). We have used pots and planters such as these for growing watercress and salad greens to make our winter diet more attractive and healthful.

Hose Watering

Now you can attach to your faucet an automatic water programmer that operates on two AA batteries. It can be set to water when and as many times as you wish. You can go on a trip with your mind at ease and know that your garden won't dry out.

MOWING
Riding Mowers

Many of us still enjoy doing some lawn mowing, even at an advanced age, and the right equipment makes it fun. For the large lawn, you can now buy easy-to-operate riding mowers with electric starters. Some of these cut the grass fine enough to be left on the turf as a mulch. Others collect the grass clippings to be deposited on the compost pile. The riding mowers have gasoline engines, and this poses a problem, because in parts of California such a gasoline engine will shortly be banned in an effort to improve air quality. Electric riding mowers are now in the design stage and may be available in the near future. Ask about them at your local hardware store.

Walking Mowers

If your lawn is not too large, perhaps it is better to consider using a walk-behind electric mower with an electric starter. There are many models and makes of these mowers, and it is worth your while to visit equipment shops and compare prices and performance before you buy.

New from Black and Decker of Canada is a much-improved and comfortable electric mower with no cord to drag around. With rechargeable batteries, this mower will cut a small lawn easily on one charge. One of the reasons this is a good safe mower for seniors is that the battery contains no liquid, so there is no leakage. What a delight to get rid of the smell of gasoline and have a quiet, non-polluting machine to give you a bit of exercise while cutting the lawn!

Muscle Mowing

As your lawn gets smaller, you can use a quiet, pollution-free machine called a reel-type hand mower. The new hand mowers are greatly improved, easy to move, never have problems with starting, and give many people the perfect amount of exercise. One company in Indiana makes a hand mower with five cutting blades for bluegrass and fescue, and a seven-blade model for the bent lawns and Bermuda grass of the southern states. If you mow regularly, leave the grass clippings on the lawn rather than bothering to collect them in a catcher. A good hand mower cuts cleanly, and leaves cuttings that decompose rapidly. The hand mower will not cut long grass, so you have to mow frequently. Look at the hand mowers in a store where you can try one out to see how it feels.

MOVING FREIGHT

There are alternatives to the wheelbarrow, which many of us find increasingly difficult to use. We have both used a common hand truck with air-inflated tires in our landscape work, and found it very satisfactory for moving such things as rocks, bales of peat, and barrels of garden debris. Many hardware stores carry these and you really need inflated tires for use on soft ground.

There are several different brands of garden carts made of exterior-grade plywood with air-inflated tires. They usually have a galvanized steel frame and a sliding panel at the front, which makes them easy to unload. Loading is also easy since you simply tip the cart up and slide things into it, avoiding the strain on your back of lifting objects into a wheelbarrow. The placement of the wheels gives the cart excellent balance and makes it very easy to move a load of 300 pounds (136 kg) or more. These carts come in several sizes, to fit your needs and your budget (32, 34).

A lighter cart of tough polyurethane is very durable and easy to wash out with a hose. Its only drawback is that it doesn't have the drop-down front for easy loading and unloading (32, 34).

GROWING STRUCTURES
Window Greenhouse

You may not have room for a lean-to or free-standing greenhouse, but a good alternative is the window

There is less chance of straining your back when you use a garden cart to move heavy objects about the yard.

greenhouse. Many gardeners find a window green-house the easiest way to garden in all seasons. You can forget about weather and heavy muscle chores, and just have fun growing plants. Try one made of resistant ther-moplastic resins — this type is very attractive, and never needs painting or other care. Two side panels open for excellent ventilation, and there is room enough for a herb garden, or fresh salad greens in pots. There is also an inside window greenhouse with ample shelves for potted plants, eliminating the problems of reaching (32).

Garden Frames

Garden frames, often called cold or hot frames, are usually installed on the ground, but there is no reason they can't be placed on a raised bed to avoid all the bending-over strain. The glazing can be polycarbonate, acrylic, polypropylene, or glass. They are available in a range of sizes, usually 4–6 feet (1.2–1.8 m) long and 2–4 feet (0.6 to 1.2 m) wide. A garden frame costs less to buy and operate than a greenhouse, and still provides enough room to grow winter salad greens.

Greenhouses

There is no more comfortable gardening for seniors and the disabled than in a greenhouse. When the snow is blowing outside, you can put on your slippers and go to see how your orchids are growing (66). New developments for the home greenhouse make garden-ing much easier for the late-life gardener. The equip-ment is now available for completely automating the small greenhouse, so that you don't have the daily chores of watering, feeding, controlling pests, and ventilating.

Many people think of greenhouses as being too expensive, but there is currently a great variety of structures available that are inexpensive season-extenders. Others, such as double-glazed heat traps, can lower the heating costs of your residence by a third.

There are many options if you decide to have a greenhouse. You should check garden magazines and catalogs to see what is available nearby. If you buy one from a company that is two hours away, you will end up paying for a lot of travel time.

The Sunshed is a combination shed and green-house that acts as a heat trap, and you will discover than on some winter days the sun provides all the heat you need. The Sunshed is the ideal place in which to do your potting and transplanting. You can improve your quality of living with this backyard hideaway, where you can listen to your favorite music, read the seed catalogs, or simply putter (32).

Somewhere near the Sunshed you should provide space for an outdoor utility room in which to put your compost facilities and perhaps a lath-roof protective area, if you have young cuttings that need shelter before going out into the garden.

Some of the models available do not require a foundation. Two people can easily erect these in a weekend (32). If you are an active senior you can get solar glazing panels and construct your own greenhouse (42).

Check the yellow pages in your phone book under Greenhouses or Solariums.

Solar Vents

Seniors often find it difficult to make frequent trips to the greenhouse or garden frame to open vents manually for cooling. We are beginning to understand how to let the sun help us garden, and the solar vent is one way of keeping the growing structure from overheating without having to watch it constantly. The vent operates by thermal pistons filled with material that expands when heated. The expansion activates a lever that opens a vent to let hot air escape. You can set the solar vent to open at 75°F (24°C) and close at 68°F (20°C), so you can leave your house without worrying about cooking your plants in a garden frame or greenhouse (42).

Solar Fans

You can let the sun turn on an exhaust fan that will push out 1400 cubic feet (130 cubic meters) of hot air per hour. This device requires no electricity and can be used in any garden structure or even in boats, campers, and vans. Again, you can adjust it to discharge at a given temperature (42, 50).

TOOL TREE

When you are working out in the garden with a whole bunch of tools, where do you put them when they are not in use? If you leave them on the ground, you will be doing a lot of unnecessary bending over and lifting.

You can avoid this by using a tool tree. It is a metal post about 6 feet (1.8 m) tall with a wire mesh basket on the top. When you are not raking, you hang the rake on the tool tree for easy access. It will also hold all the small garden paraphernalia much better than an apron or pockets. You can easily move the tool tree to wherever you are working, and into a storage shed when you are through (50).

GARDEN TOOL GRIPS

We place garden tool grips high on our list of the new ergonomic devices that make gardening easier. As we get older, our hand grip gets weaker; sometimes we get sore hands from the wooden or cold metal handles of hand tools. You can give your hands a break by using soft, durable tool grips that slide on to the handle, and stay on with the packet of glue provided. You can even use two of these on some of your long-handled tools. They come in various sizes to fit all handles (50).

ERGONOMIC GARDEN CLOTHING

You might not think of clothing as being ergonomic, but designers are helping in the fight to make gardening easier for older people.

Garden Clogs

Early spring often means wet or cold feet for the gardener working out in the thawing ground. Keep your feet warm and dry with plastic, rubber-like clogs that have a cork insole for comfort and warmth. No footwear is easier to get on and off than clogs, so you can leave them in the back hall or even outside. If you take out the insole, you can wash them down with a hose. The clogs come in nice bright colors, so you can always find them (34, 40). You can also still buy the Dutch wooden clogs, but we find them much harder to keep clean.

Gardening Pants

Gardening inevitably takes you down on your knees. To be comfortable, you need knee pads. Now you can get a pair of gardening pants with pockets inside the knees to hold neoprene foam pads. In addition, the other pockets are designed for carrying garden tools. The snap fastenings are easy to use, and the wash-and-wear fabric requires no ironing (34, 40).

Gardening Smock

A gardening smock contains all the right pockets for the gardener, has snap closures, and is roomy enough to slip on over your shirt. All you need is the proper hat to keep the hot sun off the back of your neck. We like a lightweight Panama straw that retains any shape you bend it into (40).

Gardening Gloves

In general, gardening gloves are made to look pretty and keep your fingernails clean. We have found several different kinds of ergonomic heavy-duty gloves that will let you prune roses and raspberries without tearing your clothing or your skin. They are made of new materials such as Kevlar, a compound used in automobile tires, and are tough enough to let you pick up all those rose canes you've cut off and put them in the chipper without any skin damage.

WALL FASTENERS

Many of us have had the frustrating experience of trying to drive nails into a masonry wall in order to make vine supports. You can now get what the British have used for years, a 3-inch (7.5-cm) steel wedge with a hole in the end that lets you string wires to support the plants. You can drive these into a masonry wall or a wood fence with an ordinary hammer. Run your wires and then use plant clips or twist ties to fasten the vine (34, 40).

TURFSTONES

If you require additional parking in your lawn area, but still want a green feeling, we suggest turfstones. These are patterned concrete blocks that let grass grow through the openings. This permits car traffic without adding wheel ruts, and the area can be mowed just like the rest of the lawn. From a short distance away you would never know the blocks were there — they look just like turf grass!

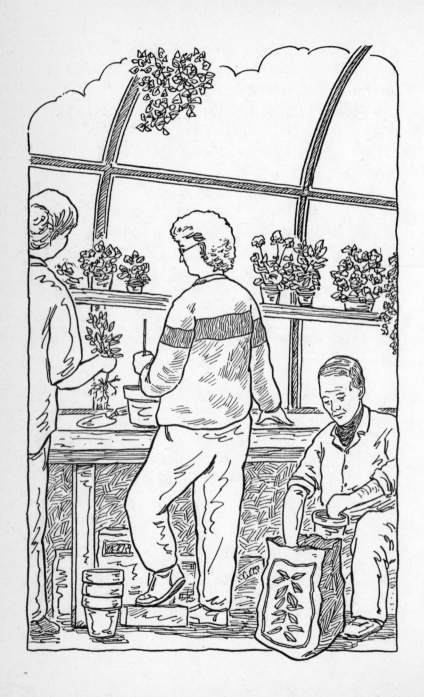

PART TWO

EASY GARDENING FOR ACTIVE SENIORS

MANY OF US ARE STILL HEALTHY ENOUGH TO CARE FOR A landscaped yard and a vegetable garden, but we don't have the stamina to spend long hours there, or lift the heavier loads that were easy when we were younger. Every year there are new products and techniques designed to make gardening easier. We have selected items that will let you keep on gardening, even though you may have to rest more often.

As you get older, you might want to consider enriching your garden experience with garden art and architecture, elements that require virtually no up-keep. If you move into an apartment, then indoor gardening presents new problems, and we will give you some ideas about reducing indoor air pollution and simplifying this type of gardening.

Sharing the joys of your garden experiences with others, in a plant society or an evening course, is an easy method of extending your gardening pleasure. And garden travel, whether consisting of tours in your area, in North America, or in other parts of the world, is becoming more and more accessible.

CHAPTER 3

GARDENING STANDING UP

GARDENING IS NOT A RECIPE YOU FOLLOW,
IT'S A RELATIONSHIP YOU LIVE.
— *Pat Stone*

Like boxers, baseball players, and other athletes, gardeners find that the first sign of body decline is in their legs. This weakening becomes apparent in the garden chores that involve balance and bending over.

Many of us have had the experience of being out in the garden, busily planting for a period of time, and suddenly standing up to find that we have a stiff and tight back. This symptom is caused by the body losing flexibility as it ages.

Experience tells us that a major garden review should occur in the middle years of the gardener's life. The children are grown and gone, and retirement is on the horizon. Your physical strength is greatly diminished. With fewer mouths to feed, the vegetable garden is probably too large. With no children at home, there is too much recreational area. Many of the foundation plants, hedges, and shrubs are overgrown. The shade trees have such large canopies that grass won't grow underneath them. At this point, the healthy senior gardener can look toward the challenge of a new garden, designed to fit his or her interests during the coming 20 years.

VERTICAL GARDENING

There are many ways to grow plants up and off the ground to avoid too much physical strain when tending them.

The vertical surfaces that will adapt to growing your favorite flowers and vegetables include frames, trellises, fences, walls, arbors, pergolas, gazebos, flower towers, and overhead shade structures. We tend to forget that you can grow vining vegetables on these vertical surfaces, including cucumbers, melons, squash, tomatoes, pole beans, peas, and gourds. You can get many of the salad green vegetables up and off the ground with vertical gardens on a fence or on casters to move about a patio.

Espaliers

The practice of espalier probably began in France, where gardening space is limited. If people want to have fruit trees, they train the trees into a fan shape against a wall, trellis, or fence. This brings the fruit to the right height at which you can prune, spray, and pick without having to stretch, reach, or bend over. You can grow your favorite fruits, such as apples, pears, grapes, or peaches, against a flat vertical surface, and so save ground space. The espaliered fruit trees are grafted on dwarfing rootstocks, so they don't outgrow the space, and if you follow the proper pruning practices they will produce abundant fruit.

In order to get a good crop of fruit, you need to use special pruning techniques for espaliered trees. In ordinary fruit trees, fruiting occurs at the ends of some branches, and the objective in pruning the espalier is to make all the branches fruit-bearing. The French, after years of experience, have developed pruning techniques for optimum fruit production on espaliers. It is worth your while to study the French method before you prune your espalier.

In colder climates, you can train your fruit trees against a southern wall, and let the heat of the sun help you have a plentiful crop.

There may be places where you would rather espalier flowers, berries, or variegated foliage. Your nurserymen can help you choose from the extensive list of ornamental plants that are available for training against a flat surface. We have used quince and camellia for flowers, and *pyracantha* for berries.

Poles, Frames, and Netting

One of the simplest structures that we have used for vertical gardening consists of chicken wire stretched between two posts. We have grown sweet peas or scarlet runner beans up to 6 feet (1.8 m) high, to work as a property-line screen. There are also various kinds of netting or mesh to stretch between poles. These materials are strong and usually plastic that will not rot or rust. You can buy such a frame ready-made at many nurseries or garden centers, or get them mail-order from a garden supply or seed company (38).

The seed companies used to be just that, selling

only seed, but today many of them have an extensive collection of garden equipment and supplies. We have found that the most comprehensive inventories are those of the garden supply companies. During the winter months when we have the time, we enjoy collecting catalogs to keep up with the new varieties of plants and products.

Trellises

You can design and make your own vertical trellis if you are handy with tools. Using your imagination to

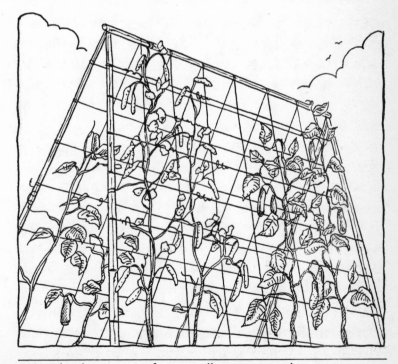

A sturdy aluminum A-frame trellis saves garden space.

design a unique trellis is a wonderful way to get a feeling of creative accomplishment. Cedar is a light, easy-to-work-with wood that lasts for a long time. The A-frame is one of the handiest types of trellis, because it needs no posts placed into the ground; it is self-supporting. You can make the A-frame with hinges, so that it can be folded and stored in the winter (32). With a lattice on one side and left open on the other, it is easy to pick heavy-fruited vegetables such as cucumber and melons. You can use mesh onion bags tied to the trellis to support individual heavy melons and squash. For smaller vining vegetables, you can cover the trellis with mesh or netting. We usually place this trellis with the long axis going east and west, and plant on the side facing the equator.

In colder climates, you can cover the A-frame trellis with polyethylene sheeting, and use it for winter protection over your choice plants, or as a row cover for early spring planting.

You can also buy all kinds of trellises ready-made, in a variety of shapes such as fans, ladders, or diamonds. Some of these are now made of high-impact plastic, fiberglass, or vinyl, which require virtually no upkeep. The important thing is to have a structure that is strong enough to support the plants that you grow on it.

Fences for Vertical Growing
Vertical gardening can be done effectively when you fasten a trellis to your wooden fence. Using a fence as part of a plant support gives you a structure strong

enough to grow the heavy-fruiting vegetables. Or you can use dimension lumber, and make planting boxes in a checkerboard pattern against the fence. If you buy or build wooden pot holders, these can be fastened to a wooden fence, and allow you a succession of blooms, from early bulbs to late fall chrysanthemums, without the back strain of weeding. Using metal brackets made for the purpose, you can even mount flower boxes on a wooden fence, and have a riotous display of color.

Walls

The only problem with vertical growing on walls of brick, stone, or masonry is making sure that you have the proper fasteners to hold your vining plants against the wall. You can buy vine supports that do not require drilling holes, and use vinyl ribbon or twist ties to fasten the plants or a wire frame to the wall. In many locations, you can also plant at the top of the wall and let all kinds of flowers, berries, and vegetables cascade down the wall.

Arbors

You can design your own wooden arbor to fit your garden. We suggest using cedar, and setting the posts in concrete for stability. If this sounds like too much work, you can buy a sturdy white vinyl arbor that requires no painting, will not rot, and is guaranteed for 20 years. You simply insert the vinyl posts into the ground, and move the arbor to various locations as you wish (28, 38).

Arbors have traditionally been covered with roses, but we have found that you can grow almost anything on them. We have had good luck with grapes and vining vegetables such as peas and scarlet runner beans.

Pergolas

A pergola is usually made of 4 x 4 inch (10.2 x 10.2 cm) posts that support horizontal rafters which cover a walk or patio. This structure is for the large home garden, and is quite often used on public buildings. One end of the pergola is sometimes connected to the building. If the rafters are spaced 2 feet (61 cm) or more apart, that permits enough light to grow vines such as wisteria or grapes. Patios or terraces usually have rafters that are 1 foot (30.5 cm) apart or less. Pergolas are best used where space isn't a problem, so the average city or suburban dweller might be wiser to consider an arbor or gazebo.

Gazebos

Gazebos come in all sorts of shapes and sizes, and are most often made of wood. You can buy kits for wooden gazebos to put together yourself, buy them ready-made, or design your own as a unique architectural feature for your property. Try some of the lumber stores near you to see what they offer.

A gazebo is a sturdy structure on which you can grow any of the vining plants. You can also sit in it for afternoon tea. (See Chapter 4 for more on arbors, pergolas, and gazebos.)

Flower Towers and Walls

As the population density increases, many of us find that there is less room for gardens, and this has prompted the use of a variety of space-saving vertical structures such as flower towers. These have the added incentive of being easier for seniors to maintain.

The simplest flower tower is a cylinder of wire mesh about 1 foot (30.5 cm) or more in diameter, and about 4–6 feet (1.2–1.8 m) tall. You line the tower with black polyethylene and fill it with a lightweight planting mixture. For economy you can easily make your own.

The easiest way to line the tower is to lay the wire flat on the ground, and fasten the polyethylene to it with twisters. Then roll the wire into a cylinder and stand it up to be filled. Before you fill in the soil, place a perforated galvanized or rigid plastic pipe in the center, one that is long enough to go into the ground at least 2 feet (61 cm) and project out the top a few inches (about 5 cm). Once the tower is filled, you can water the plants by placing a hose in the top of the perforated pipe; the pipe also keeps the tower erect. When the tower is wet, it weighs a lot, so for a first try at this keep the plant tower about 4–5 feet (1.2–1.5 m) high.

Water the tower, and then proceed to plant by simply puncturing the black polyethylene and inserting a seedling. This is a good way to get lettuce and salad greens into a vertical position. We have had good luck with some of the mini-lettuce varieties that are harvested as an entire small head for salads. Greens such as mustard, cress, and sorrel are vigorous growers, but you can harvest them young at about 6 inches (15 cm) in length. And, if you want color, you can plant a petunia tower, or almost any of the bedding plants that you wish.

There are many variations of this type of vertical garden. One of these is a plant wall built on a platform 10 inches (25 cm) wide, 4 feet (1.2 m) long and 4–5 (1.2–1.5 m) feet high, with casters on the bottom. This plant wall is ideal on a patio or terrace, where it not only provides salad greens or brilliant color, but can also be used as an outdoor space divider. If your local garden center doesn't carry such a planter, ask if they would build you one.

For your balcony, you can buy a ready-made garden storage center that is 6 feet (1.8 m) high, 4 feet (1.2 m) wide and only 18 inches (46 cm) deep. It has four shelves for displaying potted plants, and the lower shelf is ideal for storing gardening supplies and tools. It assembles easily without tools (31).

Using these plant supports will simplify cultivation and harvesting, and reduce or eliminate the weeding problem. With vertical gardening, you get better exposure to the energy of the sun for growth, and air circulation that reduces the risk of disease.

VINES

One of the best ways to have color, fruit, and berries is with vines, whether evergreen, deciduous, or annual. There are many garden books that describe vines for all kinds of climate. There are four different ways that vines stay vertical or climb.

1. Clematis and grapes are examples of deciduous vines that have tendrils that grow out of the stem and wave around in the air until they strike something. Then they wrap around any small object and form a coil spring that keeps the plant fastened tightly. You should provide a wire or plastic mesh for the tendrils to grasp, or fasten the vine to the trellis.
2. Vines such as jasmine and honeysuckle have growing ends that twine or twist about any support they touch.
3. Some vines have special adaptations, such as suction cups or rootlets, that will adhere to most vertical surfaces. Examples are Virginia creeper and ivy.
4. Most other vines must be fastened to the supporting surface. There are several varieties of snap-on plastic clips that you can apply with one hand. You can also use organic garden twine or vinyl ribbon that expands as the stem grows. For the woody vines, such as wisteria and *pyracantha*, you need a stout tie like organic twine.

The important thing when dealing with vines is to raise the foliage high enough to get the maximum amount of light, and therefore the best growth and flowering. If you plan to grow vines against the wall of a house, a common practice, you may be able to grow vines that would be too tender for exposed locations. In colder climates, the wall of the house is usually a warmer microclimate that may permit using some subtropical vines such as *Jasmine nudiflorum* and *Clematis armandii.*

HANGING BASKETS

In the past, you may have found hanging baskets hard to water. Now we have two ways of solving the watering problem. Hanging your basket with a planter pulley hanger will allow you to lower the basket to water and feed your plants, and then raise it back to whatever height you wish. A locking device on the stout nylon cord holds the basket wherever you want it. If you also use a swivel hook, it's easier to turn the basket for watering and pruning (50).

Watering is easy with devices such as the English Water-Hi, a half-gallon (2-L) plastic jug with an easy-action hand pump that will reach baskets 9 feet (2.7 m) above floor level (50). If you water with a hose, there are extension nozzles up to 30 inches (76 cm) long with thumb shut-off valves. These nozzles do the job with very little effort. As we get older, reaching is one of the movements that becomes more difficult, and devices such as these help make gardening easier.

You can buy hanging baskets made of wire, wood, or plastic. Line the wire baskets with sphagnum moss or fiber, and then fill them with potting mix. For many locations, you will find that adding a drip pan to the basket will prevent water damage to your floors or carpet. Available now are attractively designed wire baskets that consist of heavy-gauge steel painted white. These are much more decorative than the old standard florists' wire baskets (38).You can also make your own baskets out of 2-inch (5-cm) wire mesh, or chicken wire bent into a variety of shapes, such as a 2-foot (5-cm) long cylinder.

CONTAINER PLANTING

There are literally hundreds of different types of plant containers for use on the patio or porch. They are made of a variety of materials, and range from rustic to elegant in design. You can decorate with wicker baskets, hand-thrown Italian terra-cotta, porcelain cachepots, and jardinieres (31), bamboo bird-cage planters, hand-molded earthenware, enameled steel buckets, halves of wine barrels, western red cedar and redwood boxes, molded fiberglass — the list goes on and on. The best way to see what the possibilities are is to visit your local nursery or garden center or send for catalogs from the sources listed at the back of this book.

Container planters have improved a lot over the years, and are now easy to maintain. Many of these are self-watering and are fitted with an internal water well that needs attention only about once a month. For almost any size you can get a planter caddy on casters that let you move the container very easily.

On patios and porches we have often used planter boxes set up with legs, just to get the plant material to the right height for the gardener.

STAND-UP GARDENING IN THE GROUND

If you plan to continue gardening in the ground, there are new ergonomic tools that greatly reduce the need for bending over. They are described in Chapter 2.

You can now weed, feed, water, rake, dig, cultivate, aerate your compost, plant, and edge the lawn — all without bending over. You don't even have to tie your shoes anymore if you wear garden clogs!

There are knee pads, kneeling cushions, stationary stools, and a garden seat on wheels that will get you down close to the ground and your plants more easily than bending over from a standing position.

You can buy a gardener's apron much like the ones that carpenters use, to keep all your hand tools readily available and so avoid reaching and twisting.

Try some of the stand-up gardening aids described in Chapter 2. They will give your back a rest and keep it in good condition throughout your life.

SOLAR COMPOSTING

More and more cities are banning yard debris from landfills, so composting at home is becoming a necessity. We have each been composting for over 50 years, and are delighted to find a new way that eliminates the waiting, turning, and shoveling of the old compost pile. The Swisher composter is a square steel box mounted on pivots, which turns automatically to give you nice rich compost in a couple of weeks. The power comes from a photovoltaic panel mounted at one end. It doesn't take much sunlight to keep the box turning for a few minutes every day. Even on cloudy days we get enough sun energy to keep the battery charged (44).

Using the Solar Composter

You get much better compost sooner and easier if you begin by putting your yard debris and kitchen waste through a shredder-chipper, and then into the solar composter. After that, you can just use the easy-add water jug to provide moisture to the composter as it turns.

If you are starting a new compost, we would suggest that you get a package of inert decomposition bacteria from your favorite garden center and add it to the first load of organic debris. When you empty the composter, leave a shovelful of the compost to seed the next batch with the proper bacteria for decomposition. This composter comes in two sizes and the smaller takes up only 30 square inches (194 square cm) of yard space. If you don't mind the exercise, there is also a manual model for you to turn by hand.

Don't forget that there are fertilizer elements in organic debris, so that the compost you make is a good source of organic food for the plants in the garden. Nature was recycling by composting long before man arrived on the planet!

EASY CONTROL OF WEEDS, PESTS, AND DISEASE

Solarization

Most garden soils contain weed seed and a variety of bacterial and fungal spores that can be cleaned up using the energy of the sun. Soil solarization consists of covering the ground with clear plastic, and letting the rays of the sun heat the ground underneath it to temperatures high enough to kill off the weed seed, pests, and disease.

The best time to solarize the soil is before you plant an area. You can spread clear polyethylene over the ground, fasten all the edges down securely and let the sun do its work. Black plastic doesn't do as thorough a clean-up job! You should get a soil thermometer, and make sure you reach temperatures above 100°F (38°C) under the polyethylene sheet. This is an effective clean-up method even as far north as Quebec.

Recent research at the University of California lists as vulnerable to solarization 32 species of weed seed; more than 6 species of plant disease organisms; 10 genera of parasitic worms, called nematodes; and some parasitic mites. World-wide usage of soil solarization is one way of getting safe food and keeping toxic chemicals out of the environment. For more information, see the May 1992 issue of *Horticulture*.

OTHER CONTROLS

We prefer to avoid using hazardous chemicals to control pests and disease. This doesn't mean that you have to fall in love with aphids but it does mean that you should research the safer controls. Here are some suggestions:

1. Healthy, well-fed plants are less likely to have problems.
2. Look for disease-resistant varieties, especially in roses.
3. We have had good luck with liquid plastic compounds called anti-desiccants, or anti-transpirants, which are marketed under names such as Wilt-Pruf, Vapor Guard, Cloud Cover, and Anti-Wilt. The insects land on a leaf covered with this sticky stuff and get their mouthparts so gummed up that they can't chew. When fungus disease spores land on a leaf, they have a hard time getting through the waxy cover provided by these products. Give one of these a try and decide for yourself!
4. Do some research on companion planting, which helps repel some insects, and such products as diatomaceous earth and insecticidal soaps.
5. Dormant or horticultural oils have very low toxicity for humans, as well as a long shelf life. You apply these in the very early spring and the cover of oil suffocates a wide range of insects and pest and insect eggs.
6. Quite often just a strong stream of water will knock off aphids and other insects.
7. Join a garden club and find out what safe controls others are using.

CHAPTER 4

ENRICHMENT WITH GARDEN ART AND ARCHITECTURE

AND THE GLORY OF THE GARDEN SHALL NEVER PASS AWAY.
— *Rudyard Kipling*

When we reflect on the great historic gardens of Europe and the East, we realize that their enduring elements are the sculptures and architectural structures. In many ways these elements create the appeal and interest that draw generations of visitors. Trees have long life but neither the substance nor the durability of walks, bridges, or dwellings fashioned in stone. In Chinese gardens, pieces of stone and structures such as the pagoda, temple, and round moongate have priority over vegetation, and require very little maintenance. You should consider enriching your garden with art and architectural forms as well as plants.

STRUCTURES ATTACHED TO THE HOUSE
Verandas, Porches, and Porticoes
Verandas, porches, and porticoes are making a comeback. The portico is usually a few columns at the front entrance of a house, with limited space for sitting. It is

really a way to embellish the front entrance both architecturally and with plants. The porch or veranda is much larger, often as wide as the house, with ample room for porch furniture, and sometimes with part of the area enclosed to make a solarium. Many houses in the 1800s had porches up to 50 feet (15 m) long and 12 feet (3.7 m) wide — they became transition rooms between inside and outdoors.

The railings of the porch were often lined with planting boxes, and hanging baskets held plants overhead; in the cool of the evening, everyone sat out and enjoyed the view of the garden area and the countryside beyond. Very often vines such as Dutchman's Pipe or wisteria were used on the veranda for privacy. Today the front porch is gaining popularity as a refuge from the sun, where a gardener can sit and enjoy the beauty of the garden he or she has created. If insects are a problem, the porch can be screened for protection.

FREE-STANDING STRUCTURES
Greenhouses and Solariums

There are many small home greenhouses in a variety of architectural styles such as geodesic, round, hoop, and conservatory. In a circular greenhouse, the rafters radiate from a central point on the roof. This structure not only looks very attractive, but is easy to work in. In addition, there are now structures called solariums, which are usually extensions of the house in the same architectural style.

There has been a revival of interest in the conservatory, a building that can be very elaborate and exciting architecturally, if your budget permits. We discussed some low-budget structures in Chapter 2.

Sheds

Almost any shed can be converted into a sunshed simply by putting in skylights and windows through which to let the solar energy. Many great aristocratic estates of Europe and Britain had sun-filled buildings

Most sheds can be converted into sunsheds by installing skylights and windows.

that they called "orangeries" where citrus fruit was grown. There is no reason why you can't design your own sunshed to fit the surroundings where you live. This structure can have a well-insulated roof, side walls, and north wall, and still let in enough solar energy through the double-glazed south wall to grow almost any type of plant without spending a fortune on heating.

If you prefer to buy a shed, have a look at the Green Mountain Sunshed, which is architecturally a small edition of the New England saltbox house. It comes in two sizes, 8 x 8 feet (2.4 x 2.4 m) and 8 x 10 feet (2.4 x 3 m), and is made of precut panels, which can be assembled in a day. It is so pleasant that you may find yourself out there reading the seed catalogs and listening to your favorite music on a sunny winter day (32).

Scattered across North America are other companies marketing small buildings or sheds as storage buildings. Unfortunately, many of them have not yet become aware of the advantages of using roof glazing, skylights, and large windows in order to make the structure a light, airy place that will trap the heat of the sun. You can buy these sheds from many retail lumberyards or cabinetmakers in sizes from 8 x 8 feet (2.4 x 2.4 m) with no windows, to 16 x 24 feet (5 x 7.3 m) with small windows and a porch. Many can be easily adapted for storage, as well as growing plants, by adding skylights to the roof or by glazing in the porch area as a solar greenhouse.

If you did this to a model that was 10 x 12 feet (3 x 3.7 m), you would have a structure very much like that used all over Europe as a "gartenhaus." The best way to proceed, if you want a sunshed, is to look in the Yellow Pages for your area and see what is offered that can be adapted for growing plants.

Cold Frames
Even a structure as small as the cold frame can add architectural quality to the backyard garden. The one that John designed at Longwood Gardens has a pleasing architectural quality. There are arched forms and we have even seen one mounted on a raised bed so that it looks like a miniature cathedral. This is a great place to grow late winter salad greens!

A hot bed is a similar structure, but uses well-rotted manure as a base and solar heat storage units to provide heat for growing right through the winter.

Gazebos
There is a variety of architectural charm in the gazebos available at present. You can have Victorian, Oriental, or modern styles, and the structure can be made of wood, wrought iron, or vinyl — there are even canvas gazebos that you can move around to various locations. Some of the new gazebos are very light and lacy-looking, made of filigreed iron in fascinating, detailed patterns.

The gazebo is a great place to put a swim spa or hot tub that will invigorate you after gardening. The most common uses for the structure are for sitting out in the garden, and for socializing with friends over lunch or afternoon tea. You can screen-in the gazebo for insect protection and get shade from the hot summer sun.

Arbors and Pergolas

An arbor is usually a short, arched frame made of wood, metal, or plastic, which supports climbing plants or vines. A pergola is long enough to be called a semi-covered walkway. A wooden pergola offers one of the most enjoyable ways to move from the house into the garden — under the colorful drape of wisteria, fuchsia, clematis, or intertwined roses. Any of the supple small trees, such as laburnum, can be trained to grow on a pergola. You can even use espaliered fruits such as apples, pears, or grapes as a plant cover for your pergola. The end of a pergola is the ideal place to have a fountain or sculpture as a focal point to arrest your eye as you walk through. In certain places in the garden, the pergola may be curved or even a semi-circle to provide a walkway that is both functional and beautiful.

Fabric Shelters

You can now buy structures made of Monolon fabric stretched on a light aluminum frame to produce modern exciting architectural forms in a variety of vivid colors. One line, made by Enviroshade, is 10 x 10 feet (3 x 3 m) and weighs only 23 pounds (10 kg). You can move the shelter about the garden or put it over

Erecting a fabric shelter is one of the simplest ways
to have shade.

the patio, to have a decorative new way to provide
outdoor shade (43). We suspect that the architectural
charm of the fabric shelter will make it more popular
than the outdoor umbrella.

Bridges
We all seem to have a fascination with bridges. Their
greatest charm is perhaps the fact that they span
watercourses. A bridge can also be an expression of a
person or a culture.

If you want a lovely arched bridge over your waterway or pool, visit your local lumberyard and see what it offers. In some places, you can buy small bridges already assembled or in kit form. On the other hand, landscape contractors often have trained landscape carpenters who can build the bridge that you want. If your taste is for the simplicity of an Oriental bridge, you can design and build it yourself, using pressure-treated lumber that you can paint or stain to fit your landscape.

Adding a bridge to your garden can increase its charm.

The Firepit

Many people are trying to retrieve the feeling of sitting around a campfire by having a firepit, usually resting on or surrounded by a deck. Sitting by your own fire, toasting marshmallows and watching the moon rise, can be a magical experience. The firepit taps into feelings that you just don't get with a propane barbecue, and it can enrich your backyard garden architecturally. For cooking out, you can get a freestanding Tuscan iron grill for wood fire barbecues. If you build a firepit, get ready for more evening visitors than usual, because people love to sit by a fire.

GARDEN ART

Does the English garden with 100 gnomes or pink flamingos on the front lawn represent garden art, or is it just the gardener expressing his or her own tastes?

One Calgary family, the Braus, built a remarkable miniature Bavarian village in their backyard, complete with the proper small-size buildings and very attractive plantings of the right size. Karl Brau was in the bricklaying business, and when he retired he started to build the type of garden that he remembered his father and grandfather having in Germany. His skill and taste have made it a very expressive piece of garden art.

Bonsai

In recent years, many gardeners have been fascinated by bonsai as a garden art form. In milder areas, you can leave the bonsai outdoors for the winter. In northern areas where heavy frosts occur, you have to find an appropriate storage place, such as a 50°F (10°C) greenhouse, which many of us do not have. One solution is to make your own small structure. Roland successfully used a few pieces of 2 x 4 feet (0.6 x 1.2 m) lumber and some odd scraps of acrylic glazing to make a box against the south wall of the foundation of his house. He used one-inch (2.5-cm) insulation boards for the sides. For extra insurance against the cold, he put 6 inches (15 cm) of dried oak leaves over the bonsai dish.

The Sunshed is the ideal place to enjoy the practice of bonsai. More and more people are finding that there are emotional and spiritual benefits to be derived from devoting the time and care necessary to produce good dwarf plants. What is it about a 400-year-old cedar tree only 4 feet (1.2 m) tall that strikes at the heart of our feelings about plants and nature? For Asians, bonsai was a way of bringing the rigors of the high alpine areas, where nature performs its own bonsai, down into the backyard.

You can make bonsai plants a part of your **garden art** by displaying them on shelves attached to an outdoor wall, or below a porch railing. You will see people looking at them with a mixture of fascination and awe.

Sundials

The earliest sundials were probably used in Mesopotamia or Egypt. The oldest that has been found dates from 1500 B.C. in Egypt. Many cultures have used and refined them since then, and today sundials are among the most interesting of the garden ornaments.

At the Bundesgartenschau in Berlin, one of the main features is a sundial 300 feet (91 m) in diameter, which you can walk around on. The largest sundial ever built was probably one dating from 1724 in Jaipur, India; it covered an acre (0.4 hectares) of ground and had a shadow pole 100 feet (30.5 m) high.

Sundials do keep very accurate time; in fact, the early railwaymen in France set their watches by a sundial. In Egypt, there was one that had a magnifying glass focused on the wick of a small cannon, so that at high noon the wick was ignited and the cannon fired.

A variety of sundials is available, both horizontal and equatorial, to be mounted on a sculptured support. The equatorial models are often more decorative, especially as they are usually cast in bronze. The best way to get acquainted with the possibilities is to send for catalogs and then go visit a retailer.

Checking the time on a sundial once in a while seems to keep you tuned into the universe!

Man-made Sculpture
In a Fletcher Steele garden in Rochester, New York, one of the focal points is a life-size statue of a beautiful girl. The owner of the house was the model for the sculpture when she was a young woman. As the years went by, she was able to look at the statue and see herself as she had been and this helped her hold on to part of her youth. The Rockefeller estate overlooking the Hudson River is embellished by a collection of

magnificent sculptures, ranging from classic to ultramodern. Over the several hundred acres of the estate, each piece either has a setting of its own or is featured at the end of a walk or pergola.

There has recently been a tremendous increase in the variety and quantity of garden sculpture offered for sale, in forms including human figures, animals, and birds in materials such as bronze, concrete, ceramic, and stone. Very often the statuary is combined with water features. You can buy reasonably priced small statuary to use as part of a fountain. Oriental sculptural forms are now widely used in North American gardens.

The right piece of statuary is a treat for the eye, and creates a very pleasant mood in the garden. On a blustery winter day when there are no flowers in bloom, you have something beautiful to enjoy that defies the seasons.

Natural Sculpture
Asians use just a large natural piece of stone, mounted vertically, as nature's sculpture. Often this consists of an exotically shaped piece of eroded limestone, because it is available in so many places. Stones grouped together on a bed of raked sand form the Zen garden, which we would agree has spiritual overtones, since it gives you a feeling of inner peace and serenity.

Green Sculpture
The practice of pruning plants into a given shape is called topiary. Longwood Gardens in Philadelphia has

perfected the steel wire frame for topiary to produce shapes ranging from elephants to dolphins. Monrovia Nursery in California pioneered marketing the spiral forms of juniper and yew. Some suppliers are now offering topiary forms for tabletop use and even sculptures in straw (31)! There is a surprising array of living and dried plant material available for garden decoration (40).

GARDEN FURNITURE

After a long planting or pruning session, it is a pleasure to sit in comfortable outdoor furniture and just look at your garden. There is a great deal of new artistic garden furniture on the market, some of it designed by architects, which will let you convert your garden or patio into an outdoor room. You can use benches, chairs, and settees made of wood, wrought iron, aluminum, or high-impact plastic in a variety of colors. Judging by the quantity of new garden furniture, it seems evident that manufacturers expect us to be spending more time in the garden.

Wicker and willow with thick upholstered cushions bring the comfort of the living room out into the garden, complete with end tables, coffee tables, and ottoman. You can buy tables, chairs, and even rocking chairs with padded cushions for sitting comfort on the patio.

For many years residents of Appalachia have used green willow wood to make unique tables and chairs. If you buy this kind of furniture, we would suggest that you treat it with a water seal just to be sure that it lasts well. Foam cushions add comfort to this furniture, which definitely has that "hand-made," rustic look.

Bamboo
For a different look you can get rattan or bamboo chairs, tables, settees, and plant stands that are treated to resist moisture and give the patio an elegant ambience.

Redwood
Redwood has long been a favorite for outdoor furniture. A recent design places a set of modular benches between redwood planters for the patio. The natural tannins in redwood make it resistant to fungus and insects, so it stays in good condition for a long time. You really don't need to paint redwood, but you should use a clear water seal as a finish.

Teak
It is not necessary to cut all the tropical hardwood forests for wood because you can find teak furniture made from wood cut on sustained-yield plantations in Java. Teak is one of the best furniture materials there is, since the natural oils in the wood make it impervious to water, rot, and termites. The garden furniture crafted in England by the Master Craftsman Guild is some of the finest available (31).

Cedar
One of the most comfortable and attractive pieces of garden furniture is still the Adirondack chair. We

suggest that you get one made of cedar, which is weatherproof and turns a nice soft gray as the years go by.

Metal

For smaller spaces, you can buy folding metal chairs and tables with slatted wooden seats much like those that you see in the sidewalk cafés of Europe. Some of them have very attractive European beechwood for the tabletop and slats on the chairs. There is even a steel-legged trestle table large enough for the family picnic on the patio. There are also very ornate cast-iron and wrought-iron pieces, including some elegant wrought-iron rocking chairs. Period metal furniture is now reproduced in cast aluminum and will really indulge your sense of nostalgia.

Recliners

The old chaise longue has been revived for use in the garden — in white wicker with good thick foam cushions for optimum comfort. Being able to lie back and look at the sky or trees overhead is enough to make the recliner very popular. If you visit the Erholungspark in Berlin, one of the first things you will discover is that about 10,000 metal recliners have been provided so that you can lie back and watch the clouds drift over the treetops.

We have often wondered why a lot of the deck and beach furniture is not used in the garden. There is a great variety of this type of outdoor furniture, and you might want to compare costs before making any purchases. To be sure, the beach furniture is not as decorative or as well designed as some of the above-mentioned furniture, but it is probably just as good for relaxation.

The Garden Hammock
A hammock offers one way to stretch out and release your body from the pull of gravity. The new ones come with a stand and even wheels, so that you can move them around the yard. If you have any problem with your sense of balance, then a chaise longue is probably better for you than a hammock.

Entertaining
For those times when you have lots of company and need more seating, you can get folding chairs made of rust-proof resin that can be cleaned with a damp cloth, or, if you prefer, you can use plantation teak benches. The new pieces of garden furniture mean you can entertain in style.

WIND CHIMES
Many of the new wind chimes are both musical and sculpturally designed. One example has eight tubes that are tuned to the musical mode of the Gregorian chants, producing a very soothing sound; others are made of ceramic material to give you just about any kind of sound. If you like the sound of the sea, you can get one that sounds just like a bell buoy. There is such

a variety of wind chimes that you should go to see what is available near you.

BELLS
We don't ordinarily think of hanging bells in the garden, but there are some available now that are quite interesting. They are made of iron, and cast in the shape of vegetables and flowers, with a wind vane attached to the clapper so that you get clear bell tones that are very pleasant in the garden. You can have fun finding a place in the vegetable garden to hang a tomato or cucumber bell!

BIRD STRUCTURES
Houses and Feeding Stations
Birdhouses and feeding stations are becoming architecturally more attractive and colorful. You might as well add a decorative touch to your garden as you care for the birds. How about a willow wand birdhouse with a thatched roof that reminds you of Tahiti; or a hanging gazebo bird feeder; or a feeder on a stake that you put in a flower bed near the patio? There is even a squirrel-proof feeder on the market, with a spring-loaded perch so that when a squirrel (or a heavy bird) lands on it, the perch is depressed and dumps the squirrel back to the ground. You can scatter some sunflower seed on the ground so that the squirrels won't starve to death. There is such a variety that you should shop around in catalogs and at your favorite garden center to find something you like. This is certainly one

of the ways to enrich your garden area architecturally, and give yourself the pleasure of watching the birds.

Bird Baths
Another sun garden structure for bird lovers is the birdbath. The old standard concrete bowl on a stand is being replaced by birdbaths that hang in trees; some look like lotus leaves, and some are small pools with fountains that the birds love.

WATER GARDENS
Pools
One of the ways to embellish your garden is to install an in-ground pool in a secluded spot. This gives you a sheet of water that reflects the sky, to which you can add goldfish, graceful water grasses, and some of the new waterlilies, a vivid source of color and fragrance.

There is a special fascination about water plants like *Victoria regia*, with floating leaves up to 6 feet (1.8 m) across, which can be seen at Longwood Gardens near Philadelphia, and *Gunnera chilensis*, from Patagonia, which grows 6 feet (1.8 m) tall and has leaves about 4 feet (1.2 m) wide. If you have the space, you can plant the proper aquatic plants to attract waterfowl.

Installing a pond used to be a big chore, but now you can buy a complete kit with everything that you need, and hire someone to dig the shape of pool that you want. The new liners are guaranteed for ten years or more, and you can be creative with the materials that you use for a border. If you want a more permanent water feature, you can have a landscape contractor put in a concrete pool. A stream is the ideal place for one of the bridges mentioned earlier in this chapter.

Fountains

Everyone enjoys the soothing sound of water falling from a fountain or running in a stream. Your fountain can be a very simple constricted pipe, or you can pay $10,000 (Cdn.) for a cast bronze Shell Girl Fountain (inquire at your nearest garden center), depending on your budget and your taste. Once you have had a fountain, you will never want to be without one!

With a submersible recirculating pump, you are not wasting water. You simply use the same water over and over, and the pump uses very little electricity. Keep your eye open for a solar-operated fountain pump that will let the sun provide the electricity you need!

Waterfalls

People gather at waterfalls all around the world, entranced with the fluid motion of the water and all the nuances of sound that delight the ear. In nature the scale is often grand, but you can have a small waterfall in your garden area by using the same type of submersible pump mentioned above in the section on fountains. If space is a problem, there is usually enough room to have a small stream with water cascading over rock ledges.

Using natural rock for outcrops or ledges requires the expertise and equipment supplied by a landscape contractor. An alternative would be to use cast fiber-glass rocks, which are hollow and incredibly light-weight. These are castings from natural rock with the coloring done so well that seen from a few feet away you would swear they were the real thing. A waterfall of fiberglass rocks will cost far less than using collected natural rock. Try the Yellow Pages for a source close to you.

LIGHTING

Along with other garden items, you will find a tremendous variety of decorative and architecturally pleasing kinds of lighting fixtures. Some of these are less than a foot (30.5 cm) tall, for lighting walks or decks, while the post lamps go up to 8 feet (2.4 m). One type of copper lamp is shaped like a flower, and other metal lamps have a very modern style. There are even redwood box lamps to go with other redwood garden features. Most of these are low-voltage systems, and some use halogen bulbs, which are easy on the eyes.

This chapter has suggestions for added interest. New ideas proliferate faster than we can possibly record them! Visits to your local nursery or garden center on a frequent basis will keep you up-to-date with the marketplace.

CHAPTER 5

APARTMENT GARDENING

ALL GARDENS HAVE SOMETHING TO YIELD
IN THE WAY OF WISDOM.
— *Margaret Elphinstone and Julia Langley*

Many of us find that the older years are best spent in a condominium, apartment, or retirement home, to help reduce responsibilities. This doesn't mean that we have to give up our plants! You can still enjoy the fun of gardening by trying one of the following options.

- Enclose a whole balcony to make a solarium greenhouse.
- You can garden on a balcony in a mini-greenhouse, or by using moveable pots, window boxes, wall planters, and hanging baskets.
- In more and more buildings, you can garden on the roof, where each resident has a garden plot.
- Apartment residents are often assigned a garden space nearby, much like the European gartenhaus practice. The city may have a community garden where you can rent space for growing your favorite flowers and salad greens.
- You can garden indoors under lights in the utility room, or place a hydroponic tray on a south window-

sill to give you fresh winter herbs. It is even possible to do some composting.

The following are some guidelines for easy gardening in various apartment situations. A good way to find out how you can make your garden easier to care for is by doing some research in appropriate books (57, 58).

BALCONY GARDENING

Many modern apartments have balconies that can be adapted to productive flower and fruit gardening, either by enclosing the whole balcony, or by using heated benches, pots, planters, and vines.

Enclosing the Balcony

In many apartments you can get permission to enclose the entire balcony and so have another room to use for growing plants throughout the winter. Imagine sitting out under the jasmine for morning coffee. If you want completely clear glazing material so that you can look out and see the view, then use glass or acrylic sheet, which is a transparent, very tough material. John uses this for his own greenhouse, double-glazed to conserve heat and tinted so that people outside cannot see in. From inside the greenhouse the view out is just like looking through a glass window.

Acrylic sheet is not easy to work with, and it is probably best to have the work done by professional greenhouse or solarium contractors. You can even have your balcony enclosed for winter and replace the acrylic panels with screens for summer ventilation.

The enclosed balcony is really very much like a lean-to greenhouse, only up in the air. If the balcony faces the equator, you will get enough winter light; if not, you should use an additional light source. Light provides the energy for plant growth, and if you have enough light you can have fresh, chemical-free strawberries in January!

A translucent glazing will give you privacy and yet let in most of the solar radiation. Probably the best type is a new glazing material called Sun-Lite HP which is lightweight and shatterproof (42).

The Heated Bench

You don't have to glaze in and heat the whole balcony. You can make a heated bench or mini-greenhouse large enough to grow salad greens and herbs all winter. Here is how to go about it:

1. Buy or build a table the right size for your balcony.
2 Cover the table with a piece of rigid Styrofoam insulation.
3. Cover the insulation with a sheet of polyethylene, with edges tucked in so that the insulation won't get wet.
4. Over this sheet place a propagation mat that has electric heating wires imbedded in plastic and a thermostat to control the heat. This mat will keep the air above it at about 70°F (21°C) for growing almost any plant. These mats are available at garden centers and through mail order suppliers.

5. Next, make a hoop frame of arches out of split bamboo or wire, and make it tall enough to accommodate the plants you want to grow.
6. Cover the hoop frame with a double layer of polyethylene, leaving about a 1-inch (2.5-cm) space between the sheets, to conserve heat.

Now you can sow your seeds in pots, place them in the heated bench, and have a wide variety of fresh foods all winter (66). We have used this structure to grow winter salad greens such as Tom Thumb lettuce, spinach, Swiss chard, watercress, radishes, chicory, endive, chives, and a selection of herbs.

Moveable Pots
A great variety of pots are available from your local garden store — urns, cedar shrub tubs, metal buckets, terra-cotta pots, barrel halves, and very artistic porcelain jardinieres from China. Most of these can be made moveable by using an inexpensive wood or acrylic plant dolly that will hold 200 pounds (91 kg), or you can make your own dolly with casters and a wooden platform (31). Most of the larger redwood tubs, planters, and pots come with a redwood planter base that has casters for easy mobility.

Planters
Container plants are versatile, and you can enjoy them on a patio, porch, balcony, or even on a fire escape. You can grow almost any plant in a container, including

standards and small trees. In the off-the-ground locations, the limiting factor is weight, and you can solve this by using lightweight materials such as peat moss, vermiculite, and perlite for a potting soil mix. Using these materials in equal parts will provide fast drainage of water and enough air circulation for good root growth.

All sizes of planter boxes made of cedar or redwood, molded resin or ceramic, are available in both square and rectangular shapes. The best way to decide what fits your balcony is to visit garden centers and lumberyards until you find what you want.

You might like to try a Condo-Garden frame out on the balcony. These are made of galvanized steel or cedar, are easy to assemble, and give you a planting box 1 foot (30.5 cm) wide by 4 feet (120 cm) long with an overhead trellis (38).

You really don't need a variety of potting mixes for different plants. The mix described above will suit almost anything from cacti to tropical foliage plants. If you find your mix is so light that the pot tips over very easily, try adding some sand for weight.

Watering
There is no simple answer to the question of when to water plants, except to say that you water when the plant needs it. The experienced gardener watches the plants, the weather, the humidity, the temperature, and then very likely sticks his or her thumb in the pot to decide whether it's time to water. Caring for your

houseplants is much like caring for your children, in that you develop sensitivities that tell you what to do!

The most common mistake in caring for house-plants is over-watering! Keep your plants a bit on the dry side. We use a humidistat and a humidifier in the house to keep the humidity above 60%.

One word of caution for the older gardener in these days of plastic pots and artificial soil mixes! Water needs are harder to read in the artificial mixes. Experience certainly helps, but you can also judge the water needs by lifting the pot, knowing that a well-watered pot is about twice as heavy as a dry pot. A saucer placed under the pot will catch the surplus water; the new soil mixes have excellent capillary action, which will soak up the surplus.

Rail Planter Boxes

Usually these boxes are hung on the inside of the balcony rail. If you hang them on the outside of the rail, there is the danger of an object falling off. When you are shopping for a balcony rail planting box, pay particular attention to the hanging device and make sure that it is strong and sturdy. The box should be about 1 foot (30.5 cm) deep so that when you put gravel in the bottom you can then add 10 inches (25.4 cm) of soil to give your plants plenty of root room.

Be careful when you water that a lot of sloppy stuff doesn't drip to the balcony below or into the parking lot! We have an apartment-dweller friend who was planting geraniums in her balcony rail box when the doorbell rang and her minister arrived. As she ran to answer the doorbell, she left a pot of geraniums sitting on top of the rail box. About an hour later, she came back out onto the balcony and, in leaning over to wave goodbye to her minister in the parking lot below, she knocked the pot off! The falling pot missed her minister, but landed on the roof of a car waiting to take his parking space. When she paid the repair bill for fixing the roof of the car, she was sure that that was the most expensive geranium she had ever had.

Vines
You can plant annual vines such as morning glory or *Thunbergia alata* in your rail planter box and let them cascade down over the railing. You don't see these as well as the passerby does, but they make your balcony attractive.

The wall space on the balcony is the ideal place to use some of the new, attractive molded fiberglass planting boxes that are lightweight and deep enough for growing vines on the balcony (31, 32). This way you can have fresh sweet peas, fragrant climbing roses or, down south, the dramatic colors of bougainvillea. In the colder climates, you can enjoy tropical plants on the balcony all summer, and with a planter that is on casters, wheel them inside for the winter.

ROOF GARDENING
If you are high enough, and look out a window in any of our big cities, you will see acres of dirty, cluttered

roof space that could be converted into colorful gardens for the occupants of the building. If you live in a flat-roofed apartment or condominium with no roof garden, perhaps the best way to begin is to get a committee of occupants who would like to garden on the roof and go to talk with the owners of the building. Very often a roof garden means a better occupancy record for the owners.

It is very easy to use a roof garden for seasonal growing or for year-round gardening, which of course requires a lightweight greenhouse to be installed on the roof. Obviously weight is the main consideration in roof gardening, but you can buy a polystyrene soil mix that weighs only 9 pounds (4 kg) per square foot (9 square cm).

Seasonal growing on the roof is already being done in a few cities where each resident has a garden area. There is a real spirit of sharing as the residents tend their plots on warm sunny days. You can even grow small trees successfully on the rooftop. A container with 25–50 cubic feet (2.3–4.7 cubic meters) of space is enough for a 15–18 foot (4.5–5.5 m) tree to mature in. Among the preferred choices of trees are those that can be sheared, or pendulous types that are almost immune to wind damage. We have used cedars, yews, mop-head Chinese elms, and such plants as euonymus, cotoneaster, and mulberry trained to grow a single upright stem.

Some landscape architects specialize in roof garden design, and it would probably be worth your while to have one along when you go to talk with the owners.

An interesting roof garden development is Gaia Institute's Rooftop Greenhouse Project at the Cathedral of St. John the Divine in New York City. On top of one of the buildings on the cathedral grounds is a greenhouse with crops of salad greens, bulbs, herbs, and houseplants already planted. Along the inside of the parapet hang bags of compost (made from Univerisity of Columbia kitchen waste) that drip nutrients into a pipe system that carries them to the plants.

The acreage of empty flat roofs in most big cities is substantial. Recycling and growing facilities like this might well reduce the waste going to landfills, while at the same time giving seniors productive gardening activity.

Some foresight is required in scheduling the installation of a penthouse garden. Door openings, elevator size and availability should be determined before delivery of materials.

INDOOR GARDENING
If you are in a rest home or nursing home, there is still a great deal you can do with indoor gardening (60). If you would like to try something new, the English celebrate the arrival of spring with an acorn-forcing vase. This is a mini bud vase only 3 inches (7.5 cm) high that you use to force acorns, crocuses, or grape hyacinth.

Windowsills
When you visit the Netherlands, one of the first things you will notice is that very few houses have window

shades, because the windows are loaded with plants on a very wide windowsill. We have tried to get North American builders interested in broad windowsills without success. If you want to position your houseplants in an area that gets plenty of light, a plant stand in front of a window is probably the best answer. If you are handy with tools, then you can make a wide windowsill that fits over the existing narrow sill. There is also a shelf unit available that hangs from the inside top of the window, with several shelves on which to place plants (31, 32).

Plant Stands

Every year there are new plant stands on the market, in a variety of sizes and shapes. Some are made of decorative wrought iron, others are wood or plastic, and there has even been a revival of the Wardian case (named after its nineteenth-century inventor), which used to grace the parlor of the Victorian home (49). This is really a terrarium, but is also an attractive piece of furniture that will enhance any elegant living room.

POLLUTION CONTROL

Current research shows that many plants can remove gaseous pollutants from the air inside the house, and so improve the health of the occupants. Synthetic building materials and some furnishings emit pollutants such as formaldehyde, benzene, and trichloroethylene, and the right plants will absorb these toxic chemicals. You will find varieties of *pothos, aglaonema, spathiphyllum, dracaena, syngonium, philodendron,* English ivy, azalea, *dieffenbachia,* and poinsettia labelled as "Clean Air Machines" or "Pollution Fighters" in some garden shops. The soil in the pots also acts as an air cleaner. Tests are now underway by the National Aeronautics and Space Administration and the Associated Landscape Contractors of America to add to the list of plants that will clean our indoor air. The research also includes outdoor landscape plants that reduce air pollution; yucca, heather, and the common privet that we use for hedges all show great promise.

The Soviet space program has included several decades of research at the International Center for Closed Ecological Systems in Siberia. The center has developed a method of lighting and growing plants to increase the oxygen-generating capacity. This system has been tested on a small enclosed space capsule called Bios-3 and provided oxygen for three people for six months.

One of the center's scientists is now in Canada at the University of Toronto, working on a device to provide clean air and oxygen inside tightly insulated buildings and houses. The objective is to market a plant product that will sit on a shelf and, with a special automated lighting and watering system, clean the air and release increased amounts of oxygen. For those of us living in well-insulated high-rise buildings, this may mean much better air to breathe and grow plants with.

THE FOLIAGE FOR CLEAN AIR COUNCIL

The Foliage for Clean Air Council is an organization that is collecting a library of information about the role of plants as combatants of air pollution. The research on using plants to clean air is just beginning, so relatively little information is available yet about what plants absorb which of the 25 or more pollutant gases found in homes and offices. What we do know is that adding the plants mentioned above to your houseplant collection will improve the quality of air in your house or apartment.

North Americans spend 90% of their time indoors, and in many buildings the indoor air may be more polluted than the outdoor air. The indoor pollutants come from seemingly harmless things such as latex paint, solvents, rugs, upholstery, and common furnishings that we forget are breaking down and releasing chemicals into the air.

Many of us enjoy the bright red azalea (*Rhododendron indicum*) as a holiday houseplant. Research indicates that this azalea, plus the soil in the pot, will remove and completely degrade formaldehyde fumes that are in the air. The day is fast approaching when we will have a list of the houseplants that do optimum air cleaning. To keep up with the current research, you can contact Jan Roy, Foliage for Clean Air Council, 405 North Washington St., Falls Church, Virginia 22046.

NEGATIVE IONS FOR CLEAN AIR

Air is made up of molecules called ions, and the normal ratio is five positive to four negative ions.

Moving water generates negative ions by breaking up water, so that the positive charge stays with larger drops and the negative ions go free in the fine spray. Negative ions account for our feelings of well-being when we visit the seashore and waterfalls. That's one reason a shower is so satisfying and why the air seems so refreshing right after a rainstorm.

The largest negative-ion generator in the world is Niagara Falls, which may account for the fact that it is such a famous honeymoon destination, complete with lush horticultural displays (92).

Plants give off water vapor, which contains negative ions, and this may be why botanical gardens with greenhouses have become so popular lately. Not only are the plants beautiful and fragrant, but the air is invigorating, a nice change from city air.

We both keep many houseplants in our homes, as well as negative-ion generators. Most of the particulate matter in the air, such as smoke and some airborne bacteria, is positively charged; the negative ions attach to these to render them neutral, making them fall to the floor. This is one way that plants clean indoor air. We have set a negative-ion generator on the edge of the table at bridge games where people smoked, and have found that the air stays smoke-free (35).

GARDENING UNDER LIGHTS
Gardening under lights used to be quite a chore, but now there are completely equipped gardening-under-light plant stands available for your tabletop (32), or

two- and three-shelf stands on which you can grow a great variety of plants.

Light provides the energy that drives plant growth, so it is important to grow your plants under a light source that comes closest to natural outdoor sunlight. For a long time, commercial growers have used cool white, warm white, and incandescent lamps to provide as much of the light spectrum as possible. You can buy improved lamps for growing that provide about 90% of the natural sunlight spectrum (32). You should replace the fluorescent lamps at least once a year to get the maximum energy output for good growth.

Natural sunlight is about 10,000 foot-candles, but a lot of this light in the yellow and green range is not used by plants. Plants do use the far-red, red, blue, and violet waves. Plant lamps are designed to provide just the part of the light spectrum that the plants use. For growing with artificial light, you need at least 100 foot-candles for the foliage plants. For the plants that produce flowers or fruit, you need about 1000 foot-candles of light.

Some plants will survive at 50 foot-candles, but they don't grow! At almost every cocktail party we go to we are approached by someone who asks what's wrong with the philodendron in their living room. The answer is usually that there is not enough light available to provide the energy for growth. If you have houseplants that are not doing well, try adding light sources and you'll be surprised at how much better your plants will grow.

You need a light stand that takes two fluorescent tubes and lets you adjust the light source to fit the plants you are growing. The best of the new stands come with heavy-duty plastic trays in which to set your pots or seed germination trays. In the colder climates, germinating seed under lights is one way to get a head-start on the spring season. You can also grow a wide variety of houseplants from seed. We both enjoy forcing bulbs, such as paper white narcissus, amaryllis, and dwarf daffodils, to get that early spring feeling!

Tabletop gardening can be done inside, using fluorescent lights.

Most plants respond well to 12 to 14 hours of light per day. The best way to determine the proper light time is by watching your plants and experimenting. You can learn many skills by joining one of the Light Gardening societies and sharing experiences with the members.

COMPOSTING

If you are living in an apartment you can still have nice rich compost for your potted plants or window garden by using a kitchen composter under the sink. We tend to think of indoor composting as being messy and smelly, but the new indoor composting boxes will turn kitchen vegetable scraps, shredded paper, and even hair into an odorless compost, rich in earthworm castings. The secret is the right worms — one of the best is the African Night Crawler (*Eudrilus eugeniae*). There are farms that raise these worms and sell them by the pound or kilogram. The earthworm castings absorb odor so well that they are even used as kitty litter! Try these new indoor composters not only to get a prime ingredient for your potting soil, but also because you can help reduce the deposits at landfills, which have a high content of kitchen waste. Ask at your local garden store.

This advantage of composting has been recognized by some cities with landfill problems. In Toronto, you can call the City Works Department and get a reduced price on a kitchen composter, along with a book called *Worms Eat My Garbage*, by Mary Appelhof. Call your own city authorities for such a deal!

HYDROPONICS

One of the things that we both enjoy is going into a garden shop where we can talk to an owner who has been in the business for many years, and who knows the solutions to most of our problems. Consequently, we often go to FMCI Hydroponics in Burlington, Ontario, because the owner, Frank Pastor, Jr., is knowledgeable, and also manufactures his own hydroponic equipment (30). You can probably find such a supplier of hydroponic equipment in the Yellow Pages for your locality.

Hydroponic growing, or soilless gardening, has been going on for a long time and is practiced widely in everything from space capsules to nuclear submarines, and from the deserts of the Middle East to the barren cold of the Arctic. The Hanging Gardens of Babylon were hydroponic!

Our object here is to help you get acquainted with an easy method of indoor gardening all year round. We have both enjoyed growing a variety of salad greens and herbs this way for many years.

There isn't any one type of system that is better than all the others, so you have to decide what you want to grow, how much space you have, and what fits your budget. We have both grown hydroponic food on south windowsills, using the appropriate equipment, all through the winter, and nothing tastes better than a salad of freshly picked watercress grown without any chemical treatment.

Using the proper lights, you can turn your utility

room into a food factory. When spring arrives, move your hydroponic unit out onto the apartment balcony to get natural sunlight. In the United States, Hydro-farm Gardening Products, with four locations across the country, sells an excellent lighted hydroponic garden (33).

The best way to get started is to read up on the subject in a good book (64). We have recommended Stewart Kenyon's *Hydroponics for the Home Gardener* because it is complete and easy to read; he has owned his own hydroponic company and has had a lot of experience with people doing hydroponic growing.

You will find it helpful to talk to other people who are growing hydroponically, and the easiest way to do this is to join a society (10, 18).

CHAPTER 6

SOCIAL GARDENING

THOUGH AN OLD MAN, I AM BUT A YOUNG GARDENER.
— *Thomas Jefferson*

Man is a social animal, and gardeners are certainly no exception. Few occupations or hobbies offer the opportunity to literally enjoy the fruits of others. Who hasn't traded shoots, seeds, or even a share of his or her garden harvest with another? This, of course, is only the beginning of sharing between gardeners, and it can extend to advice, instruction, and even assistance throughout the community. From informal neighborhood networks to membership in organized groups, clubs and societies, the chances for social contact abound!

When you grow the largest pumpkin or win a prize at your local garden show, you get an immediate boost in self-esteem. This is your reward for the creative exercise of raising an amaryllis to full bloom or growing a tree from your own rooted cutting. Sharing your garden experiences with someone who is just beginning makes both of you feel good.

When gardeners share information about their crops, they are improving their communication skills. Most beginners can gain helpful tips from conversations with other gardeners in a social setting — when two gardeners meet at a cocktail party, what do you think the small talk is about? Gardening provides the subject matter for comfortable social intercourse.

There are all kinds of organizations and activities, including garden clubs, plant societies, night courses, field trips, flower shows, fairs, tours, and botanical gardens and arboreta, where you can explore horticulture in a relaxed social atmosphere. Helping your children learn to garden can create a family intimacy that is often difficult to reach. Sharing an activity can strengthen the family unit.

BOTANICAL GARDENS

We would like to do a little explaining about botanical gardens and arboreta. Roland recently retired as director of the School of Horticulture at the Niagara Parks Botanical Garden, and John was on the staff of the New York Botanical Garden. With this background, we should be able to help you understand more about these institutions.

Many experts attribute the first botanical gardens in Western civilization to Renaissance Italy; these gardens primarily featured medicinal plants. Over the years, the botanical garden has developed four main functions.

The first is to collect plants from all over the world and grow them where everyone can see them on display. Second is to do research, which involves preserving gene pools, hybridizing, and genetic engineering for new plants or new plant properties. Third is to maintain an herbarium, which is a reference collection of dried plant specimens available to help gardeners identify plants. If you don't know what the plant is, you won't know how to grow it! And fourth is to provide information for the public and the professional practitioner. A lot of the educational value comes from the display gardens where you can go to see the various kinds of plants that you may want to use.

Botanical gardens have such a spectacular riot of color during the growing season that they have become prime tourist attractions. Parks have a limited variety of plant material, and stress recreation rather than education.

Today botanical gardens have become much more accessible to the general public. No longer considered musty plant museums, they now present an infinite variety of programs that are entertaining, educational, and participatory. These programs are dependent upon the services of the many amateur gardeners who volunteer to help fund and operate the gardens and do it because they have a lot of fun!

The best botanical libraries are in the older botanical gardens and arboreta, as well as in conservatories that draw people all through the year to enjoy spectacular displays of color. Many of the older conservatories are now being restored, as public interest in them increases. There are also new, very modern "climatoriums," containing everything from rainforest to desert, to help people understand the global environment.

ARBORETA

An arboretum is a collection of trees or woody plants maintained for professional research purposes and for public use. Quite often an arboretum is associated with a university, and becomes an outdoor laboratory for the study of trees. Collections of trees in cemeteries, parks, and golf courses are also called arboreta. Sometimes the trees in these collections are labeled to help the public get to know the different types. Many arboreta publish the results of their research in bulletins.

FIELD TRIPS

Field trips provide one of the best social gardening experiences, because there is a definite holiday quality to climbing on the bus for a visit to a botanical garden. John taught night courses for many years, and always found the students ready and willing to omit a week-night session in order to take a Saturday field trip.

In attending international horticultural events, we always sign up for the field trips early, because they get filled rapidly. At one such congress in Leningrad, John signed up for a trip to Tajikistan, where he met and set up a seed exchange with Academician Ovchinikov, a member of the Soviet Academy of Science. John sent him a pound of California redwood seed, and told him he would like to live to see the slopes of the Himalayas covered with redwoods. When John was about to leave Tajik, he told Ovchinikov that he would write. In reply Ovchinikov passed him a pen, which John later discovered had a 22-carat-gold top. The Tajiks were hungry for world contacts. Taking field trips is a way of expanding and sharing your garden interests and knowledge.

SHARING YOUR GARDEN

Once your garden is in good shape, you'll have fun sharing it with other gardeners. One of the best ways to make new gardening friends is to have an Open Garden Day (much like an Open House Day) or a Yard Show (instead of a Yard Sale). Your friends see your garden all the time, so it is fun to let the general public in to have a look. With the new friends you make, you'll get to see many new gardens. Liz Primeau, editor of *Canadian Gardening*, has tried this with great success and the magazine now offers free Open Garden signs to subscribers. We think this idea will become very popular, because gardeners have a strong curiosity about what their associates are doing.

HORTICULTURE AS A HOBBY

Horticulture is really a thousand hobbies! Just think of the many fulfilling tasks you can do, such as rooting your own cuttings or watching seeds germinate. It is satisfying and enjoyable to learn how to reproduce a plant that you prize. The reason that there are so many plant societies is that people enjoy talking about this hobby, and sharing their experiences with everything from African violets to roses or orchids.

Innovative gardeners all across North America have created garden beauty against horrendous odds. For example, last summer we visited Calgary, Alberta, where we found a splendid private hillside garden facing the Rocky Mountains. The garden was a tribute to Evelyn Salamanowicz, who has a business career, is a housewife with family, and still finds time to garden. Her neatly labeled rose garden is exposed to the winter chinook winds that cause the temperature to either plummet or rise 50°F (26.5°C) in an hour! She uses straw and truck tarps for winter protection. This may not be your concept of easy gardening, but avid gardeners will do anything to keep their garden growing. While the winter wind is blowing outside, Evelyn, wearing her shorts and slippers, takes care of a basement full of African violets under lights.

Joining a garden club is a good way to get acquainted with the many aspects of horticulture that you can adopt as a hobby. You might be interested in food gardening, flower arranging, exotic bulbs, or even hybridizing new varieties, but get familiar with the scope of horticulture before you make a selection. In the process, you will acquire a host of new friends with whom to share your gardening adventures.

It is easy to underestimate the value of plants to all kinds of people. We do have a subliminal awareness of our relationship with plants — this is shown by the way we use plants to mark our most important rituals, from the cradle to the grave.

Hybridizing

There was a grape farmer who, at the age of retirement, realized that the Concord grape was coming to an end as a wine-making grape. He had been growing Concords for years, and as he went up and down the rows, he kept noticing that one plant had thicker leaves and a more robust growth. He selected this plant and, after propagating many more from it, found that he had a grape with three times the sugar content of the Concord. He patented it in the United States under a number.

Roland's friend Rudy Behring specializes in breeding alpine rhododendrons from China and the Himalayas, and has many new varieties registered with the American Rhododendron Society. His hardy varieties have made it possible to have rhododendron gardens in places such as the Montreal Botanical Garden, where the winters are too cold for many plants. And Rudy's plants travel around the world! He grows them in Niagara, Ontario; they are propagated at Clay Laboratories in British Columbia, grown to maturity in Japan and New Zealand, and sold in Britain, France, and Spain. This is a hobby for Rudy, who works as a Bell Telephone technician.

You can get so interested in horticulture as a hobby that you may become another Luther Burbank, a plant breeder who developed countless varieties of fruits and vegetables, and who in 1921 wrote an eight-volume treatise, *How Plants Are Trained to Work for Man*. Over the years, many other hobbyists have bred new varieties, and many today still find this a fascinating challenge. You get a special kind of satisfaction out of creating a new plant variety for everyone to enjoy.

Collecting

If you go to England, visit Allan Bloom's nursery in Bresingham and see his collection of alpine plants. Allan has traveled all over the planet, collecting wild species of alpines and bringing them back to cultivate at his nursery. It is a fun place to visit, because Allan's new hobby is collecting steam locomotives. You can ride around the 200-acre (81-hectare) nursery in a little carriage hooked up to a big locomotive. Allan Bloom's plants are now being distributed in North America, so ask for them at your local nursery.

If you are still able to travel and hike, collecting is one of the most enjoyable plant hobbies.

Flower Arranging

Flower arranging is one of the horticultural hobbies that you can pursue well into your advanced years. All kinds of flower shows and fairs feature plant arrangements and run contests for the best creations. This hobby can also develop into a business. After all, it *is* the basis of the florist industry. From wedding flowers to all the arrangements that are used as decoration for home, church, and social affairs, flower arranging will give you ample opportunity to express yourself and raise your sense of self-esteem.

This is just a sample of the many aspects of horticulture that make excellent hobbies. If you join a garden club, you will get to talk with people who have found an absorbing hobby and are delighted to share it with you.

FOREIGN TRAVEL

Area parks and gardens have long been popular destinations for family and social outings. With the more sophisticated travel services available, and the increase in time enjoyed by seniors, garden tours to neighboring states or provinces are also becoming commonplace. For the more affluent and/or physically able, exotic garden tours can be taken yearly with professional tour guides capable of revealing the history of Kew or the great royal gardens of Europe. Even the secrets of the Oriental gardens of Suzhou, Kyoto, and Djakarta can be discovered on the right tour.

For those with a bent for travel, the whole world is available. This is the era of the garden holiday, tour, or vacation. Europe has enjoyed for many years the Floriade, the Bundesgartenschau, and similar events. These can be likened to the "Olympics of Horticulture," and actually involve competitive displays of horticultural excellence. In recent years, major cities in Germany, France, Belgium, the Netherlands, Italy, and other countries have hosted such exhibits, usually at four-year intervals.

The 1985 Bundesgartenschau at Erholungspark in Berlin was a good example of the scope of some of these displays. More than 20 landscape professionals worked for ten years to construct a unique park on 300 acres (121 hectares) near the Tempelhof Airport. Some of the notable features of the park include a lake and streams with 15 different styles of bridges, a sundial 300 feet (91 m) in diameter, horticultural architecture, a great number of benches, and several thousand recliners, which allow you to lie back and look at the sky. If walking is a problem, you can take the narrow-gauge railway and tour the entire park, stopping at the various attractions.

There are 20 theme gardens, including gardens to attract birds, bees, and butterflies. Displays show all kinds of paving, wall construction, fencing, arbors, and trellises, to give you a host of new ideas about what to do in your own garden. The Karl Foerster perennial garden, with more than 300 species, is a memorial to one of Germany's famous horticulturists. In the Exhibition Hall, you can see displays of flower arranging, bonsai, flower sculpture, and a variety of seasonal plant shows.

A visit to one of these international plant events is exciting, rewarding, and a lot of fun if you are an avid gardener. Unlike the Olympics, the displays are frequently open for a six-month period. Montreal was the first North American venue for a "Floralies" in 1980. To commemorate the 500th anniversary of Columbus's voyage, Columbus, Ohio, presented a similar event, the "Ameriflora" in 1992.

Preparation
Advanced planning is the secret to trouble-free enjoyment of foreign garden tours. The best way to accomplish this is to find a good travel agent. Like so many other service businesses, travel agents vary in their talents and experience. It is wise to ask a prospective

agent about the last foreign tour he or she arranged. Ask for the names of several of the people who went on the tour, and talk with them about how well it was organized.

You need a current passport that will not expire while you are overseas, perhaps a visa, vaccinations for various tropical diseases, medical insurance, and documentation of your own physical condition. If you are on medication or have allergies, a physician in a foreign country might need to know about them.

A recent innovation is IAMAT, the International Association for Medical Assistance to Travelers. Here's what they have to say in their brochure:

> IAMAT has secured more than one hundred acres of property within one hour's drive of Niagara Falls. With the support of donors around the world a complex designed as the home of IAMAT will be erected. Here both physicians and laymen from throughout the world will come to study and coordinate medical services for the benefit of travelers who need medical attention on their journeys (19).

Another helpful association is MAPP, Medical Assistance Passport Plan, Inn Care of America Inc., Box 1204, Clarksville, Tennesee. You can get a brochure from them that explains the program. It is designed to help you cross borders with a generous supply of pills. Customs people are very drug-sensitive, and when they find your pill supply you'll get through much more quickly if you have the correct documentation from your physician. You have to plan for an ample supply of hearing aid batteries, contact lenses or glasses, denture adhesive, and any other helpful items that you normally use.

A good travel agency knows all about the food, clothing customs, and the seasonal weather of the country you will be visiting. Even with very careful planning, there can be surprises. When Roland went to the Baja Peninsula, looking for the giant cactus (*Pachycereus pringlei*) and the Boojum Tree (*Idria columnaris*), he encountered varied weather. He slept out along the coast one night when it was 93°F (34°C) and the next night was a few miles inland and had frost. As Mark Twain said, "If you don't like the weather — wait a minute!"

One big advantage of the conducted tour is that the tour agency provides experienced gardeners or horticulturists as guides, and quite often uses local experts and interpreters. Some of the best of these tours are conducted by the staff of botanical gardens.

Garden travel, whether on a local or a world-wide basis, can add immeasurably to your enjoyment of life. In many parts of the world, the great gardens and landscapes usually coincide with the most popular tour agendas. The old adage "He travels fastest who travels alone" may be the golden rule when you're in a hurry, but it certainly isn't the approach to use in garden study or appreciation. Touring with a group or a companion can broaden your vision and your learning experience. We have covered many international horticultural "high spots" (and some amazing backwaters), and have found that two heads are better than one in perceiving and establishing viewpoints and conclusions.

Check on the laws about bringing plants from the tropics into the United States or Canada. You may find that the safest procedure is to bring in only seeds.

NORTH AMERICAN TRAVEL

In eastern North America you can reach a diverse collection of parks, gardens, and ornamental landscapes in a single day by car. In spite of the pressure from population growth and pollution, many of these gardens provide lush green vegetation and horticultural variety to charm the visiting gardener.

Climate, the creator of all growth, has not changed significantly in the last 500 years, and Canada and the northern parts of the United States still have the successive seasons of garden display. The heat and humidity of summer alternate with winter dormancy, interrupted briefly by the instant vigor of spring growth and the exotic colors of autumn, to give northern gardens four refreshingly different landscapes. This sequence is almost impossible to duplicate in the rest of the world.

In less than a week, you can drive from the east to the west coast of North America. On the west coast, you will find the world's tallest trees, the redwoods, which grow up to 300 feet (91 m), and the oldest trees, the bristlecone pines, some of which may be over 5000 years old.

Up north is prime temperate rainforest, and in the south are some of the driest deserts in the world. In between are fertile valleys with dramatically varied horticulture, ranging from poinsettia plantations to macadamia nut farms, with a galaxy of residential gardens echoing virtually every garden style known.

There are more than 500 botanical gardens and clubs across North America where you can get help with the particular climatic problems of the area where you live. For example, the Millarville Horticultural Society in Calgary, Alberta, details the garden techniques required for the chinook area of Alberta, in its book *Gardening Under the Arch*.

GARDEN TRAVEL HELP

The Garden Tourist is a useful new travel book that lists, state by state, all the garden and flower events across America. One of the most exciting things about many of the tours listed is that you are given access to private gardens all over the country; this is the only way you will ever see some of these spectacular spaces.

In the back of the book there is an extensive list of the foreign garden tours that cover all the flower and garden events in Europe. As on the American tours, you are given access to many estate gardens, where you can not only meet the owners, but are often invited for tea (15)!

LATIN NAMES

Don't let the Latin names of plants scare you! There is a good reason for Latin names, and they really are not much more difficult than many of the names of the diverse people who inhabit the earth. The reason for using Latin is that it is a common language for anyone working with plants around the planet. For example, you know exactly what you mean when you say "Creeping Charlie," but to someone in Texas the same plant might be "Moneywort" or "Creeping Jennie." A Chinese gardener would not understand you at all. If you were to use the Latin name, however, you could write to a seed company in Texas or a friend in China and ask if they had *Lysimachia Nummularia*, and they would know exactly what plant you meant. So the dead language of Latin lets plant people cross the language barrier and communicate clearly. The first name is the genus, much like the family name for humans, and the second name is the species, like the individual name for a person.

The Latin name is quite often taken from the person who first found the plant, and it can also be descriptive of some part of the plant. *Hosta*, for example, is named for Nicholas Hosta, an Austrian physician who found the plant while traveling in the Far East in the late 1700s. *Lobelia* is named for Mathias de Lobel, who brought the Cardinal Flower to the court of King James I. And many plants have a species name of *latifolia*, which means "wide leaves."

Once you begin using the Latin names, you'll find them easy, and it will improve your stature as a plant person. For very little money, you can get a plant book called *Plant Names Simplified* that tells you how to pronounce the names and what they mean.

Professionals use a 1000-page book called *Hortus III*, which is full of plant names accepted world-wide. The people who classify and identify plants (and animals) as a profession are called taxonomists, and they all begin in the botanical gardens where the reference collections are kept. John was at one time a taxonomist at the New York Botanical Garden and worked on keeping Britton and Brown's *Illustrated Flora of the Northern United States and Canada* up to date.

Any classification of nature is really for the convenience of man. For example, when taxonomist Wendell Camp was at the New York Botanical Garden, he was employed by the blueberry growers to classify eastern blueberries. He worked on this for several years in the field. When he finished, he had to tell the growers that while he could distinguish a blueberry species in Maine from one in New Jersey, in the area where the two populations overlapped on Cape Cod, the blueberries were all one species. That's nature!

COMPETITIVE GROWING
As you gain in gardening expertise, you may discover the world of competitive growing. When you are a beginning gardener, you probably spend a lot of time

visiting other gardens, private and public. As you begin to see results in your own garden, however, you will no doubt be encouraged enough to receive the visitors who gave you guidance just seasons ago. With a little success, the competitive spirit will move you. European gardeners have a long tradition of growing vegetables to enter into the local annual fair. Without a doubt, the major attraction of these contests is the fun that the gardeners have in trying to outdo each other, and the sharing of gardening information and tips, such as how to grow the heaviest cabbage.

Whether it's for the Great Pumpkin crown or the prize for the most fragrant rose, you will probably find an opportunity to compete in one of the many categories of exhibits in your local flower show. As your gardening efforts reach maturity, you may be inspired to enter your entire landscape in contests such as the Ontario Trillium Awards or a similar landscape competition in your own area. Our experience indicates that your new friends and admirers will greatly outnumber any "poor losers" or enemies that might cross your path.

Many gardeners soon develop a passionate interest in one particular flower, shrub, tree group, or plant requiring special skills. Examples are roses, lilacs, rhododendrons, cacti, succulents, and many others. In fact, *Gardening by Mail*, by Barbara Barton (52), has a five-page listing complete with addresses and telephone numbers for specialized plant societies.

ENVIRONMENTAL ACTIVITIES

Equally fascinating, but requiring somewhat different skills, are numerous new activities connected with today's environmental concerns. They include the Big Tree Hunt, in which you seek out the largest, rarest, or most historic tree in a given municipality or location. The Heritage Forest in the United States is a program for developing tree collections from genetic duplicates of famous trees in history with propagation by seeds, tissue culture, or other methods. The program is fostered by the American Forestry Association.

The Forestry Association of Ontario has for many years maintained the Ontario Honour Roll of Trees. Many of our friends and associates have contributed notable entries to this listing. As the years pass, new discoveries can displace the original entries, for size and general merit. Other movements, such as Global Releaf and the Green Environment, also present exciting opportunities for the gardener to participate in activities that are relevant to our concern for the environment.

NIGHT COURSES AND WORKSHOPS
Evening Courses

Many schools and colleges offer night courses in various aspects of horticulture and landscape design. When you attend these courses, not only do you learn how to garden, but you can also meet all kinds of people with whom to share your enjoyment of gardening. John taught evening courses for 30 years, and discovered that the new students learned from the older, more experienced gardeners as well as the teacher. Often people taking the course seemed to be there to find a suitable mate for marriage! This confirms that the classroom is for social intercourse as well as learning.

Workshops

Most botanical gardens (and some schools) have practical workshops, usually held on Saturdays. The benefit of workshops is that you usually have time to do much more than you would in a night class, and you can accomplish tasks in the daylight at a botanical garden that are not possible at night in a classroom. A workshop is a "hands-on" experience, where you get to do pruning, bonsai, or grafting, rather than just learning about the subject. Workshops usually have no more than four sessions, compared to the eight to twelve meetings of a night course, and quite often they are held on successive days like Friday, Saturday, and Sunday. There are even botanical gardens that offer noon-hour nature walks for the harried business worker.

Helping Others Garden

Every botanical garden could use more volunteers to help with their programs. When you teach a child how to plant seeds or root cuttings, or show someone with severe physical limitations the joy of handling plants, you get a feeling of satisfaction that is indescribable. It is similar to what we feel, as authors, when we share our lifetime of experience with you, the reader.

COMMUNITY GARDENING

At Your Apartment

In many cities or towns, apartment owners will provide garden space, on the property or elsewhere, for the residents of the building. Sometimes there is even a greenhouse attached to the apartment building, for the residents to use. If you live in a building where no garden space is available, it might be worthwhile to talk with the owners.

In Germany, the garden spaces for high-rise dwellers are on the edge of town, and are large enough to allow each resident to build a small cottage, known as a "gartenhaus," on his or her plot. The apartment-dweller gardener goes out to his or her gartenhaus for the weekend, grows fresh vegetables, and shares a lot of social fun and gardening with his neighbors. Throughout Germany, you will find that almost every town has a gartenhaus village. North America might well adopt this idea for improving the quality of living for high-rise dwellers.

Some North American cities either provide or rent garden space on city property. It is certainly worth your time to call city hall and find out if such a service is available. Many botanical gardens or arboreta sponsor community garden programs. Contact the one nearest you, or try some of the places listed in the Sources.

For Your Community

Numerous opportunities are available in most North American cities for participating in community enrichment projects. Whether you live in a small town or in a major metropolitan area, there is bound to be a gardening project underway that needs leaders and volunteers.

Anyone familiar with New York City is aware that the South Bronx contains some of the most devastated areas of urban decay that can be found. This area is changing as the result of the "Bronx Green-Up" program initiated by the New York Botanical Garden under the direction of Terry Keller. They now have more than 150 community gardens, on abandoned lots that were covered with garbage and every conceivable kind of trash. Each garden is an oasis producing flowers, fruit, vegetables, and above all, neighborhood pride.

Improvements of this kind can affect whole sections of a city, and tend to put a stop to littering and vandalism. Botanical gardens are overseeing this kind of urban rejuvenation in other cities as well, so you should be able to find a program that can use your help.

One of the major nursery-stock growers in Ohio, Lake County Nursery, is also busy as a catalyst for volunteer town-beautification projects. Talking with James Zampini, the president of the company, we realized that it is often the drive and enthusiasm of one person that makes these projects successful. For over 20 years the town of Painesville, Ohio, in the "rust bucket" northeast, had suffered a drastic decline in community pride and morale. James was able to start several beautification projects, from small civic properties to the local college campus, which improved the attitude and morale of the residents. The work was done by volunteers from all levels of society, all races, ages, and physical abilities, who all earned a new feeling of pride in their community. James has his own 3P formula for urban beautification, People–Plants–Paint!

Projects such as these are happening all over North America, and you will find it rewarding to give them your support. Here in Ontario we have garden clubs, horticultural societies, and park departments engaged in many different beautification activities. Volunteer to help with the projects going on in your community, for your own personal satisfaction and for the benefit to your city.

PART THREE

CHANGING GARDEN DESIGN AS YOU AGE

MOST OF US HAVE HAD MANY YEARS OF GARDENING ON OUR own property, with no limitations to worry about, but there comes a time when the wheelbarrow is too heavy and the lawn too large. This is the time to consider redesigning your existing garden for low maintenance and maximum safety. We will consider ways of adapting your home landscape to fit your physical condition and your budget, your options for redesign by professionals, and your options for having professional construction and maintenance. We will suggest ways to enrich your garden experience with artistic features such as sculpture and fountains. You never have to prune a sculpture!

CHAPTER 7

GENERAL DESIGN FOR ALL CONDITIONS

WHETHER WE KNOW IT OR NOT, ASPECTS OF CONTEMPORARY
LIFE PLACE THE GARDEN WITHIN A BROADER SPECTRUM
THAN THAT CONTAINED BY THE GARDEN WALL.
— *John Brookes*

In the adaptive garden design the aim is to make the changes necessary to fit the senior gardener. Possible changes include:

1. Safe, well-lit walkways and paths for easy traffic, both for people walking and those using wheelchairs.
2. Raised beds and planting structures that make garden care easy, even from a wheelchair.
3. Enrichment with color, texture, sound, garden art, and ornament, to add interest, but not work, to the garden.
4. Appropriate varieties of plant material that are disease-resistant and require minimum attention.

THE NEW AMERICAN YARD
A new garden ethic is reaching homes all across North America, as people try to make their properties healthier, more pleasant places to live. Dr. Henry M. Cathey of the U.S. Department of Agriculture has called his

approach to home property design the "New American Yard." As the former director of the U.S. National Arboretum, with his wealth of diverse experience, Dr. Cathey has become the spokesman for all the plant-related industries and is a fountain of ideas.

Dr. Cathey's concept of the New American Yard includes design criteria such as:

- Planning an all-season display to keep something happening in the garden year-round and to increase the diversity of plants used. The average yard can display as many as 100 different varieties of plants.
- Using plant selection to eliminate from the design both the dull species and those that require a lot of pruning, and fostering those that have dramatic seasonal displays of leaf, flower, and seed head.
- Choosing tough plants that will resist drought, require less watering or feeding, and need only limited use of pesticides.
- Reducing care chores both by using plants that require attention only once a year, in the early spring clean-up, and by mulching to conserve moisture and cut down on the need for weeding.
- Considering nature as a guide for planting in natural groupings that fit the planting location.
- Using soil management to provide the proper pH, organic content, and moisture retention in the root zone.
- Changing the role of the lawn to emphasize function, rather than having it simply fill space. The lawn

can have a design shape of its own, be a series of green walkways through planted areas, or be divided into small intimate relaxation spaces.

The New American Yard has enough lawn to reap the health benefits of recycling water, absorbing pollutants and heat, and moderating climate. Many of these new design ideas are on display at the New American Friendship Garden at the U.S. National Arboretum in Washington, D.C.

DOING YOUR OWN REDESIGN

If you have some talent at the drawing board, then you can plan the changes you want to make and have a landscape contractor come and do the work under your direction. You certainly know your own problems better than anyone else, and you may well be the best person to adapt your garden to fit your condition.

Another possibility is to use the technique of many Asian landscape architects, who do not draw plans at all but design directly in the garden, where they can visually check their ideas. Many people don't have the kind of mind that easily converts lines on paper to mental pictures. We have both done landscape design for clients who had no idea what the garden would look like from seeing it as a line drawing!

GETTING DESIGN HELP
Your Local Nursery or Garden Center

In our experience, the best way to begin planning your

redesign is to visit your favorite nursery or garden center and talk with the manager or owner, preferably on a quiet weekday when he or she has the time to give you advice. Most responsible firms know that it is in their interest to offer the service of helping you with your garden plans. The nursery may provide a planning service for a fee that is refundable when you purchase materials. The distinct advantage of getting help locally is that the staff will be familiar with your climate and handy whenever you have other garden problems. Your garden center is also usually a good place to pick up helpful information sheets as well as garden products.

Just as the seed catalogs now have excellent directions for growing plants, some nursery catalogs have added complete sections on planning your garden. For example, the catalog from Sheridan Nurseries in Georgetown and other locations in Ontario has a planning section that includes line drawings of sample landscape plans in different stages, as well as instructions on how to get your plan onto paper. This section also gives information on landscape materials, tells you how to select trees and shrubs from plant lists, gives hints for maintenance, and includes a plant-hardiness zone map to insure that you don't lose plants to cold winter weather.

Design Books
In many landscape design books the authors speak of garden design in lofty, abstract terms, somewhat

incomprehensible to the average gardener, and they use examples that are alien to our current life-styles. Get a copy of a book with a simple, direct presentation of what garden design is all about. Our recommendation is a book by John Brookes (54). In a few short pages, he is able to give a clear presentation of the key ingredients in garden design: shape, proportion, balance, and composition. In addition, he brings a keen insight into matters of color, inspiration, and the devices necessary to create appropriate solutions to the problems of both urban and rural property. His book will help you get started on the mechanics of making a plan for your garden. Understanding a few basic design principles prior to consultation with your professional will greatly assist your deliberations.

Other Design Help
Look into the possibility of taking an evening course in landscape design at a botanical garden or school, or plant to visit one of the many botanical gardens that have landscape gardens on display. By seeing what others have done, you will gain some idea of what you want to incorporate into your own property design.

For $1 (U.S.) you can get a Yard and Garden Remodeling Kit from the Garden Council (14). If you have never done any landscape design, don't let the prospect scare you. A lot of the design process is just good common sense, and creating a garden that suits your physical condition will give you pleasure. The kit makes the design process easier than starting from scratch with just graph paper.

Here in Niagara-on-the-Lake, our friend Campbell Scott did his own landscape design so successfully that he has had color photo articles in at least six magazines, and has been featured on several television garden programs.

PROFESSIONAL HELP

If you just don't feel comfortable trying to redesign your own garden, you should contact a professional with the specialized training to give you what you need. There are at least three types of professionals who can do adaptive planning for you.

1. Landscape architects have extensive training in all types of landscape and garden design, as well as horticulture, and many of them are now using techniques that will let you see your proposed new garden on video. The landscape architect comes to your home and films your present garden or landscape on videotape. He or she then takes this back to the office and puts the tape into a computer. Using the proper software the architect can redo your garden, putting in new trees or decks and taking out and moving around other features, all on the computer. Then he or she will put several new designs onto the videotape, and bring them for you to view on your television screen. You can sit in the comfort of your living room and redesign your garden!

Most landscape architects have had training and experience in ergonomics, and can help provide the tools, equipment, and garden arrangement that best suits you. In any case, before making any decisions, be sure to see work that the landscape architect has done, and talk with people for whom he or she has designed.

2. Landscape designers and contractors are often very talented and could be exactly who you need for your redesign. Again, the key to success is to see any adaptive garden work that the firm has already done, and to talk with previous customers before making a decision. It is likely that many of the adaptive changes you will want to make will require heavy equipment, for example, for paving, stonework, carpentry, and moving large trees. This is where you need a good landscape contractor who has the skills and the equipment for such heavy-labour jobs.

3. Horticultural therapists have three levels of professional expertise: horticultural therapist, horticultural therapy technician, and Master's horticultural therapist. If you have decided not to tackle redesigning your own garden, then a Master's horticultural therapist has the skills to do adaptive garden design and give you a new garden that suits your physical ability. The changes can involve adding ramps, raised beds, ergonomic tools, easy-care plants, and anything else you need to make your senior years of gardening a real pleasure.

COMPUTER DESIGN

We both use computers for word processing and find them easily accessible. If you have a computer, there are a number of software programs available for designing your garden on the computer screen. The advantage of the computer is that you can do all kinds of experimenting and changing on the screen and even watch the plants grow and change color with the seasons! Many software programs have a substantial plant database, which is a big help in selecting the right plants for the right location. You'll find these programs are a lot easier than trying to draw plans on graph paper, and they give you a sneak preview of what your garden will look like.

In the March/April 1992 issue of the *National Gardening* magazine, there is an evaluation of 21 different software programs that assist the gardener in designing. We would suggest that you read this article if you are interested in using your computer for planning your garden.

One of the largest databases is the CompuServe Network, which has a program GO/Garden run by the National Gardening Institute, and a Gardening Forum that lets you contact other gardeners and share information by modem. If you are just getting acquainted with plants, the plant-finder programs will be of special interest. Computer software is not a replacement for books and catalogs, but it can provide a wealth of information.

COSTS

It is wise to decide how much you can afford for your adaptive garden design before you begin contacting different companies. Most professionals like to know what the budget restrictions are, so that they can choose the adaptive garden solutions to fit the budget. You really need price quotations from two or three sources in order to compare costs for design, and your budget should also include the construction costs. Very often the professional designer can suggest several solutions (representing a range of costs) to your garden problem. You can then choose what suits you and your budget best.

The Low-Budget Garden

Many urban gardens are being redesigned by landscape architects and contractors who can deliver a mature landscape that looks as though it had been there for years, if you can afford the price. For most of us there are, fortunately, other options available.

You can start with small plants. A tree seedling in a 1-gallon (4.5-L) pot may cost a dollar or two. The older the tree, the more it will cost. You can stretch your landscape dollar by using small plants; frequently the smaller plant adapts much better to a new location, and the risk of loss is minimized.

Even greater savings are possible if you grow your plants from seed and cuttings. You can produce hedges, perennial borders, and various trees, with simple propagating equipment that is widely available.

You can begin with a few ground-cover plants and divide them every season to cover more area, rather than buying enough initially to fill all the space.

There is a wide selection of geraniums and bedding plants that you can grow from seed at much less cost than buying the plants. As you grow more plants from seed, you will have some extras to trade or exchange at your local garden club or plant society. We enjoy attending yard sales, auctions, and flea markets to look for low-cost garden equipment. Above all it pays to shop around for most goods and services, because prices *do* vary in location and time!

LIGHTS

The gardens of many seniors lack adequate lighting. There are now several different lighting systems available that make the garden safely accessible at night. Some of these are solar-operated and will charge their batteries during the daylight to give light for the garden after sundown. Other systems are 12 volt, which cost very little to operate and can provide a delightful play of light and shadow, as well as safety. A good way to get acquainted with the types of lighting available is to go to the library and look through the current garden magazines.

TREES IN THE GARDEN DESIGN

Without a doubt, the single most important element in your landscape is trees. Trees provide shade, flowers, and fruit; clean and cool the air; and give us a feeling of protective comfort when we sit under their canopy of green leaves. So it is important to select the variety of trees that fits the size of your property and meets your needs. Perhaps the best way to do this is to visit a botanical garden or arboretum, where you can see the adult size of a wide variety of trees. They are usually labeled, so you can become familiar with the names of the trees you wish to select. It is worthwhile to acquire some knowledge of tree characteristics. Your selection can depend on many characteristics — color and richness of foliage, time and quality of bloom, the nature of seed and fruit. Some characteristics you may consider negative, such as odor, continuous litter, obtrusive roots, or hostility to other neighboring trees. Many of the current nursery catalogs list the merits and drawbacks of the trees they market and they tend to stay away from the trees that cause problems.

The two most important considerations are the hardiness zone in which a tree grows well and the mature size of the tree. In the older parts of many cities, properties where the trees have outgrown their location are a common sight. When the owners planted a nice, little 4-foot (1.2-m) evergreen at the corner of the house, no one told them that it would grow to be a 100-foot (30.5-m) forest giant!

On the basis of a lifetime's work with trees, we would like to make some suggestions for your tree selection. We have both had the experience of going back to landscape sites where we planted young saplings and seeing huge shade trees with trunks nearly 2 feet (61 cm) in diameter!

Shade Trees
These are the trees, called deciduous, that lose their leaves in the fall. They are usually the first consideration for the designer when preparing the planting plan. Commonly used are maple, beech, oak, linden, locust, elm, tulip tree, sycamore, and birch.

Don't overlook the elms! There are now hybrid elms that are very disease-resistant! An elm in Central Park has survived disease, pollution, and climate for 120 years. This tree has been cloned, and thousands have been planted in the New York City area with great success.

For the past 20 years, the Elm Research Institute has been working with clones of these tough old American elms that survived the epidemic of Dutch elm disease. Now they have the Liberty elm ready for distribution to municipalities and individuals. During this decade, they hope to have a million new Liberty elms planted where other elm trees used to be. To obtain trees, you can contact the Elm Research Institute, Harrisville, New Hampshire 03450.

Many people are bothered by the trees that drop their leaves, seeds, fruit, and flower petals all over the lawn. The best answer to this is to plant your deciduous trees in flower or ground-cover beds, so that everything that falls lands in a planting bed and provides a mulch, rather than debris in your swimming pool. This is exactly what happens in a native wood-land managed by Mother Nature!

Other people are delighted to sweep up leaves for compost and to have apples for cider, and pine cones for the fireplace and Christmas weaths. Using the correct body movement and the right ergonomic easy-gardening tools, you may find these chores easier than you thought.

Some maples and beech offer dense shade, while the locust, gingko, and birch provide filtered sunlight that is more compatible with underplantings. You want summer shade on the patio and house, so the proper shade trees will be on the south or west in our northern hemisphere.

Native Trees
If you plant the native species of trees, they will grow better than some of the highly bred varieties because they are adapted to the environmental conditions where you live. You will find specimens of native trees in most botanical gardens. Quite often you have to hunt for a nursery or garden center that stocks native plants, but it is worth the effort.

The Evergreen Trees (Conifers)
We are all familiar with the pine, spruce, fir, hemlock, cedar, and their relatives that make up our forests. In northern climates, the yearning for greenery in winter is common, and the evergreen trees give us a feeling of green throughout the year. These trees also provide

winter habitat for birds and give us windbreaks, some shade, and screening for year-round privacy.

The evergreens affect senses other than the visual. Who has not enjoyed the whisper of wind in the pines or the aroma of balsam fir? And no group of trees requires such minimal maintenance while giving us so much in beauty, symmetry, and movement. Most of our conifers are extremely long-lived, and they offer more shades of green than any other plant material. Selected forms of spruce and fir produce a broad range of blue, silver, and gray foliage, which makes excellent specimen plants and focal points.

Evergreen trees will shed much less debris on lawn surfaces than those that lose their leaves. But it is still annoying to find your light hand mower trying to grind up pine and fir cones, so plant the evergreens in flower or shrub beds. There are also the evergreens that, like the deciduous shade trees, shed their leaves every year. These include the larch or tamarack (*Larix*), the bald cypress (*Taxodium*), and the dawn redwood with the dandy Latin name, *Metasequoia glyptostroboides*! Don't let the Latin name scare you — the tree is beautiful!

Virtually all of the conifer species have developed numerous dwarf and other unusual forms suitable for the smallest garden. When you are selecting trees, be sure to find out the mature size of the one you like, and if the planting space is restricted, use one of the dwarf forms. A whole new industry has developed to provide these smaller evergreen specimens, and you may well find a nursery in your area that specializes in dwarf evergreens.

FLOWERING TREES

This is another loosely defined category of trees, which embraces a wide range of specimens deserving use in every garden. Their outstanding merits include foliage color, attractive blossoms and fruit, and a wide range of shapes, including fastigiate, pendulous, globular, mounded, and topiary. They range in size from grafted standards no more than 4 or 5 feet (1.2 or 1.5 m) tall to larger varieties up to 25 or 30 feet (7.5 or 9 m). This diversity lets you fit more than one type into any garden situation.

Flowering Crab Apples

Some of the larger wholesale nurseries, such as Lake County Nursery in Perry, Ohio, are very active in developing new hybrids. They currently list over 20 new hybrids of flowering crabs, including weeping and columnar forms, some of which you will find in your local nursery. The Amaszam flowering crab has bright red flowers in the spring, maroon foliage all summer, and orange fruits for nearly all winter. How's that for garden color?

Ornamental Pears

Several new ornamental Callery pears are grown for their white flowers and brilliant fall foliage; a special series is hardy in northern areas. One of these is the

Valzam pear, which is labeled a "Carefree-Maintenance" tree. The best way to get familiar with the new developments in flowering trees is to find a good nursery in your area that keeps up with the times.

In the taller range of flowering trees you can provide shade where oaks and maples would be too large for the site. Some varieties that we like are hawthorn, Oriental cherry, lilac, magnolia, Kashmir mountain ash, flowering almond, dogwood, Chilean firebush, yellow wood, fringe tree, silk tree, golden rain tree, sorrel tree, myrtle, red jade apple, purple-leaved plum, Japanese maple, and Osage orange, to name just a few. Tree roses are gaining in popularity every year, and are just the right height for easy care in the stand-up garden.

You should become familiar with the hardiness of these flowering trees, because some of them don't do well in northern zones. The nurseries near you usually carry the varieties that are hardy in your area. To get acquainted with the best varieties for northern gardens we suggest a book we mentioned in the previous chapter, *Gardening Under the Arch*, published by the Millarville Horticultural Society in Calgary, Alberta. The dedication of the book says it all: "To all who garden in spite of Jack Frost and Johnny Chinook"!

Many nurseries have color catalogs of all kinds of plant material, and if you make a collection of these it is a liberal education in what you can have in your garden for fruit, flower, and foliage color.

FRUIT TREES

For the limited space of the average garden we would suggest the dwarf apples and pears. The dwarf apples are grafted on a Malling rootstock, which slows the growth of the tree so that you can harvest a crop without ladders. These trees are not self-pollinating, so you have to plant two varieties in order to get fruit. There is no substitute for biting into a fresh Red Delicious apple or a Clapp's Favorite pear from your own backyard.

NUT TREES

Just up the street from our office is a member of the Society of Ontario Nut Growers, who has his yard filled with nut trees. We tend to forget that the nut trees are nature's gift to the gardener — they provide shade, color, and food, with very little attention. New hybrids of pecans, chestnuts, walnuts, filberts, and heartnuts are doing well even here in Ontario. If you would like to add some to your adaptive design, get in touch with the Ontario Nut Growers or the Northern Nut Growers Association in Ohio.

SPECIALTY GARDENS
Dried Flower Garden

Many gardeners would like a special garden for growing the plants that make attractive arrangements for the house when they are properly dried. Once cut, you simply hang the flowers upside down in bunches away from sunlight, and at room temperature. Slow drying gives much better results than hanging them over a heat source. Here are some suggestions for your dried flower garden:

Yarrow flowers in white, yellow, rose, and red.

Wild Onion will provide flowering heads in lavender pink to reddish purple. There are about 500 species in the wild and 20 species available in nurseries.

Artichoke has spectacular bluish-purple flowers that dry well for arrangements.

Safflower has bright orange-yellow flower heads.

Cockscomb has flowers that are pink, orange, crimson, and gold to add color to winter bouquets.

Globe Thistle has blue flowers that hold their color when dried.

Sea Holly has large blue bracts around the flower head that last well when dried.

Strawflower will give you shades of yellow, orange, red, pink, or white.

Statice has bicolor flowers.

Bells of Ireland gives you green flowers.

Quaking Grass (*Briza*) has straw-colored, pendulous seed spikelets for arrangements.

The Herb Garden

Of all the specialty gardens, the herb garden is riding the highest crest of popularity at the moment. This is no doubt an expression of our efforts to return to nature and a healthy life-style. Earlier civilizations cultivated herbs for a variety of uses related to the medicinal, culinary, and cosmetic arts, and even for more lethal purposes such as deadly poisons. The early botanical gardens were predominantly herb gardens.

Growing herbs in your own garden requires some basic decisions about use and design. You have to consider the ultimate size and growing pattern of the particular herbs you want to grow. Some, such as dill, dock, and lovage, grow tall and rank, and might best be planted in the vegetable garden or in front of a shrub border. Some tall plants, such as lavender, can line the driveway as part of the landscape planting. If your only need is mint for your rack of lamb, plant a clump near the back door and jump back quickly — it is a fast grower! Smaller herbs such as thyme and parsley will do well in a design herb garden.

Beautiful herb gardens have traditionally been geometric, such as the knot garden that has been used in Europe for centuries. The geometric shape is composed of an intricate woven pattern of clipped and manicured plants such as *Teucrium*, *Santolina*, and *Alternanthera*. The herbs are then planted inside the geometric design and the total effect is very attractive.

FERNS
We have both used ferns extensively on our own home properties and in landscape development for others, so we feel confident in recommending that ferns be considered one of the landscape plants that belongs on every property. For shady areas nothing beats the graceful green of a generous cluster of

ferns. In planning your redesign, you might well define all the shade areas and use ferns there as the primary planting. You can add other shade plants for a variety of shapes and shades of green.

If you haven't done much with ferns, perhaps the best way to get started is with a good book. The book we recommend in the bibliography (59) is tailored for the beginner and tells you how to collect ferns in the wild and how to use them in your own landscape plantings. Long before the dinosaurs roamed the earth, there were hundreds of species of ferns, including tree ferns that are still used as landscape specimens in subtropical North America. Perhaps one reason that the ferns have survived so well is that while most flowering plants produce seeds by the hundreds, one fern will disperse spores by the millions.

You can also use ferns as houseplants. There are more than 25 species of tropical ferns that make enchanting, care-free houseplants. We are all familiar with the Boston fern, which will drape from a hanging basket down 3 feet (91 cm) or more and is produced for sale by the hundreds of thousands. Once you are familiar with ferns, you can visit nearby greenhouses and garden centers and select some to use in the house.

LIVING IN THE GARDEN
Utility Room and Shed
The garden is really an extension of the house, and the proper design techniques can make it as functional and comfortable as your indoor rooms. One of the

rooms that adds to the efficiency of a house is the utility room, and for the outdoor garden this function is usually fulfilled by a utility shed. It is not difficult to remodel an existing shed and make it a solar shed by removing part of the solid roof and replacing it with glazing that lets the sun in. This not only makes the shed a place for storage, but enables it to be used as a garden workshop for potting plants, starting seeds, and growing winter salad greens. If your shed is made of wood, you can convert it into a solar shed by installing skylights and wall windows. You can also buy kits with which to built your own solar shed. The Sunshed we mentioned earlier acts as a heat trap and you will find winter days when the sun provides all the heat you need. Everyone enjoys the right kind of place to do potting and transplanting, and the Sunshed is ideal. You can improve your quality of living with this backyard hideaway, where you can listen to your favorite music, read the seed catalogs, or just putter (32).

Somewhere near the Sunshed you will need to provide space for an outdoor utility room to put your compost facilities and perhaps a lath-roof protective area, if you have young cuttings that need shelter before going out into the garden.

Cooling Off

What is more refreshing than a dip in the swim spa or hot tub after a session of pruning, weeding, or mowing the lawn? One of John's relatives built a gazebo, and inside installed a swim spa that fits 6 to 8 people comfortably. This swim spa has water jets that allow you to swim in place, or you can turn them off if you want to just lie back and relax. Adjacent to the swim spa is a deck with a firepit, and the combination of the two makes a Saturday at home feel like being on holiday. And no water is wasted, because when you drain and change the water in the spa it goes into the garden. Lots of fun for family and friends!

We tend to think of this kind of equipment as being expensive, but there are now preformed fiberglass and redwood spas and hot tubs that are quite reasonable.

Yard Shower
If your budget won't stretch to build a swim spa, then you can install the new Gardena garden shower anywhere in the backyard. It comes with a spike that you stick into the ground and attach your hose to. The shower head has a stainless steel filter that is easy to clean. You can move the shower around anywhere in the garden where you want water on the plants (43).

Activities
There is a sense in which the backyard garden becomes an outdoor recreation room, and you can liven up your social life if you adapt your garden for entertaining. It is also enjoyable to show off what you are doing in the garden.

In Europe, many people live in the garden every weekend during the season at their local gartenhaus village (see Chapter 6). They stay in a structure much like the Sunshed except that it includes a hammock or two for sleeping. They spend their time both gardening and visiting, because it is a short walk from cottage to cottage. We have visited several of these gartenhaus villages and have been amazed at how quickly the signs of stress disappear in a social gardening atmosphere.

CONSERVING WATER

We should all be adapting our gardening to use less water. As a result of the drought conditions in some parts of North America, we now have improved equipment and materials designed to let us grow plants as well as ever, but using less water.

Watering Container Plants

There are half a dozen companies now marketing polymers (chemical compounds) that will soak up and hold water in the soil so that you don't have to water as often. You can go away on a hot weekend and come home to find your outdoor pots showing no signs of wilt. Watering less often certainly qualifies for the easy lifelong gardening designation, while at the same time conserving our water supply.

One of the best ways to use polymers is to put approximately a tablespoon into 1 gallon (4.5 L) of warm water and let the granules absorb water overnight. Then pour off the excess water and mix the hydrated polymer granules sparingly into the soil. You have to experiment with how much to use for the particular size of pot. If you use polymers in a raised bed, do the mixing before you plant. If you put unhudrated polymers into a pot and then water, you are likely to find the potting soil coming up over the edge of the pot and making a mess.

Two of the brand names you might look for are Terra-Sorb and SoilMoist, and there are others which you will probably find at your local garden center (41, 45).

Rainbarrels
The old-fashioned rainbarrel is making a comeback — it makes good sense to save the rainwater run-off from the roof and use it to water the garden. The new rainbarrels are made of molded polyethylene that won't crack or chip, with a spigot so that you can easily fill a watering can. Some models are quite attractive, and it is satisfying to be conserving water.

Xeriscaping
This is the term used to describe landscaping that will let you reduce your water use by 50% or more. Many people like Karen Kees of Poway, California, have had their allocation of water severely reduced by the city. Karen didn't give up gardening; she still has an attractive colorful garden that uses much less water. Here are her suggestions:

1. Group your plants according to their water needs.
2. Use drought-tolerant plants. Most of these have gray foliage, but bloom in gorgeous colours.

3. Use mini spray heads that keep the water close to the ground.
4. Use self-watering pots or drip emitters for container plants.
5. Apply a mulch of about 3 inches (7.5 cm) to keep moisture in the soil.
6. Add some garden ornaments that enrich the garden but use no water.

OTHER GARDENS
It is not our intention, in this book, to consider all the types of gardens that you might use for ideas in designing your adaptive garden, but to help you get started in having a garden that is easy to maintain and that suits your condition. You will probably use flowering shrubs as a background for perennials, bulbs, annuals, and border plants. You may want a rock garden, pool and water lilies, vines, or a vegetable garden for pesticide-free food. The best way to include some of these gardens in your plan is to start with a book like John Brookes's (54), and then explore other books in the bibliography. In addition, you should join a garden club and get access to the wealth of experience that other gardeners have accumulated.

CHAPTER 8

DESIGNING FOR THE PROBLEMS OF AGING

PRIVACY IS ONE OF THE MOST VALUABLE AND ONE
OF THE RAREST OF COMMODITIES.
–*John Ormsbee Simonds*

As we age, we want a comfortable sheltered garden that is quiet and pollution-free. We want to do less work and avoid stooping, bending, reaching, and lifting. Free of the routine of employment, we have more time to spend in the garden and want to be comfortable as we enjoy our relaxation and rest.

THE LAWN
The time has come to reassess the role of the lawn in home landscaping, keeping in mind the pleasure of attractive, easy-to-maintain grounds, and the need for a setting for family life, for games, and for sports.

Designing Your New Small Lawn
The lawn is usually the largest surface area in your yard, and requires weekly attention in the form of mowing, feeding, weeding, and control of pest and disease. If your budget permits, you can have someone come in and do the maintenance, but this deprives you

of the exercise and the good green feeling of gardening.

One of the things you will want to do is to make your lawn smaller to reduce the time and effort involved in caring for it. When you do this, give some thought to having a lawn given a definite shape by putting a concrete walk, about 2 feet (61 cm) wide, around the perimeter. This makes the mowing and edging much easier, and at the same time is aesthetically pleasing. Usually a lawn is a ragged pattern of green that is left over after you have put in all the flower beds, but it is pleasant and refreshing to see green turf in a well-defined shape. This keeps the grass from growing into the flower beds, and with a good mower you can eliminate having to edge the turf. You can move more easily around the garden on a level surface with a wheelbarrow or cart.

To make gardening as well as maintenance of the outside of the house easier, we once put a 2-foot (61-cm) walk right against the foundation of a house. It went all the way around, and planting was then done along the outer edge of the walk. The residents could either get into the back of a wide flower bed or paint the house without having to do battle with a host of plants. When you looked at the beds you hardly noticed that there was a concrete walk behind them, because the eye stopped at the vivid color of the flowers in front of the walk.

Historical Background on the Lawn
Long before the advent of mowing equipment,

grasses played a significant role in human habitation. The earliest lawns were probably found in Scandinavia, Northern Europe, and the British Isles, where the right temperature and humidity helped evolve so many of our turf-type grasses. As traffic and grazing affected the lush greenery of the native grasses, the first lawns were created. Early use of this space was probably mainly for games, since by the Middle Ages, golf and lawn bowling had appeared, necessitating a closely sheared turf. In North America the dominance of the forest made a tremendous impression on the immigrants from Europe. The lawn as we know it was introduced only when there were well-established villages; the grazing animals did the lawn mowing.

Lawn Facts

- There are 30 million acres (12 million hectares) of turf in the United States.
- Installation and care of lawns is a $25-billion-dollar business employing half a million people.
- A lawn has 6 plants per square inch (6.5 cm²), 850 per square foot (92.9 cm²), or about 8 million in the average 10,000-square-foot (9290-m²) lawn.
- Noise levels are reduced 20–30% by lawn areas.
- Air temperatures are 30°F (22°C) cooler over lawn grass than asphalt, and 12°F (6°C) cooler than over bare soil.

One of the first companies to make a lawn mowing

machine is still in business after 150 years in Ipswich, England. The extent of the time we now spend mowing lawns has become enormous and, in fact, excessive. Since the move to suburbia that accompanied the surge in car ownership in the twentieth century, many of us are having second thoughts about maintaining large areas of lawn. But grass or turf *is* an environmental asset, which helps to keep your home landscape a healthy place. Although most of the oxygen in the air comes from plankton in the ocean, some comes from lawn grass and trees. Turf also acts to cool the air by releasing from the leaves as much as 10,000 gallons (45, 460 L) of water per acre (0.4 hectare) into the air on a hot windy day. Besides, it feels good to walk across the lawn in your bare feet!

EASY-CARE VARIETIES OF GRASS
Background
At the end of World War II the discovery of a superb, vigorous, dark green strain of bluegrass in Merion, Pennsylvania, spawned a new turf grass industry — commercial sod production. The root mat of the grass was formed of interlocking stolons, which made it possible to roll up sections of sod. This discovery, along with the introduction of selective weed killers and the increased availability of nitrogen, catapulted Merion bluegrass into a dominant position in the North America lawn industry. By 1980, lawn care had become a half-billion-dollar-a-year business in New York State alone. Instant lawns for instant homes had arrived.

Environmental concerns are now prompting turf specialists to look toward grasses with lower energy demands, more resistance to drought, and less need of chemical control and constant care. All of these characteristics are of interest to the senior gardener.

Existing New Varieties
Our fifty-year love affair with bluegrass is far from over. Many of the excellent cultivars will still play a major role in home landscape and commercial sod production for many years to come. There are now about 200 new varieties of lawn grass being introduced, and they fall into three categories:

1. *Perennial Ryegrasses*
   Perennial ryegrasses are derived from the old familiar common ryegrass, long used as a component in lawn seed mixes to provide quick germination and fast cover. The new cultivars have finer leaves, greater density, better shade tolerance, and are more resistant to pests, disease, and extremes of hot and cold. They will also tolerate lower mowing.
2. *Fine Fescues*
   Fescues have the finest leaves of any turf grass. They may be used in pure stands or in mixtures, and are excellent for overseeding existing turf. They have the lowest fertilizer demands of any cool-season grass, are drought resistant, and will enter summer dormancy when water is withheld.

3. *Tall Fescues*

The tall fescues are another group of fine fescues noted for their excellent root development. They make better use of soil moisture and mineral nutrients than any other lawn grass. They are quite tolerant to mowing and a wide range of soil conditions.

We recommend that you go to your favorite garden center for advice on these new cultivars. For more detailed information, you can contact The Lawn Institute, County Line Road, P.O. Box 108, Pleasant Hill, Tennessee 38758.

Buffalo Grass

New grass varieties may eventually reduce the amount of water, fertilizer, and mowing that are needed to have a presentable green lawn. Buffalo grass is one of the varieties that the University of Nebraska will market as soon as it is patented.

Over the past seven years, research on native buffalo grass has been underway at the University of California at Davis, and has resulted in the Highlight varieties that withstand drought, require less water, grow to a height of 4–6 inches (10–15 cm), and need mowing only two or three times a year.

Under the direction of Lin Wu, professor of Environmental Horticulture, the research team collected specimens from Mexico to North Dakota in order to crossbreed for the right characteristics. The Highlight series will be available to the trade in about two years.

We both feel that the benefits of lawns are so substantial that everyone should have one at home and every city should provide many in the urban environment.

Meadows as Alternatives to Lawns
A movement has grown up recently to replace some lawn areas with wildflower meadows. There may be some large areas where this approach is beneficial, but problems can arise with a meadow on the home property. A botanical garden in New York experimented with the wildflower meadow and found that, after a few years, the single sowing of wildflowers had been replaced by common weeds, and the colorful panorama that we all enjoy in meadows was gone.

Many states and provinces have weed acts that make it illegal to grow some of the pernicious varieties that may show up in a seed packet. It is difficult to clean seed so thoroughly that there is zero weed content in packaged seed.

Perhaps a better solution is to have the proper turf around your residence and enjoy wildflower meadows on holiday. We shouldn't forget that the green feeling we get from nature comes as much from turf as from flowers.

GROUND COVERS
Over the years various alternatives to lawns have been proposed, and many have merit, but not to the total exclusion of grass. There *are* ground covers, however,

that are much better adapted to certain environmental conditions than turf grass.

Ground covers consist of any low perennials, shrubs, or sprawling vines that hug the ground, spread rapidly by runners, and require little or no maintenance. By low, we mean plants from 1 inch (2.5 cm) to 3 feet (91 cm) tall, such as some of the ferns that do very well in heavy-shade areas. It is important to select those that make a tight, solid, evergreen cover.

Over the years we have used many kinds of ground covers, and would suggest that those listed below are among your best bets for problem-free alternatives to turf. The first six are old standards used around the world. We heartily recommend ground covers as one of the ways to make lifelong gardening easier.

Easy to Grow
English Ivy (*Hedera Helix*) There are many forms, and you might like to try a variegated variety called "Gold Child" as ground cover in shady locations. This received an award of merit from the Royal Horticultural Society. Available from Ivies of the World, Box 408, Weirsdale, Florida 32695, and Merry Gardens, Camden, Maine 04834. These ivies will grow under shrubs right up to the trunk of a tree.

To get some color we have often planted clematis in the ivy bed and let it sprawl unsupported. You can do the same with other vines that bloom well.
Myrtle (*Vinca minor*) Certainly among the best of the ground covers, this 6-inch (15-cm) plant thrives in sun

or shade, and sends out long trailers that root as they go. The flowers are white, purple, or blue, and one form has variegated leaves.

Japanese Spurge (*Pachysandra terminalis*) This is one of the most widely used 6- to 8-inch (15- to 20-cm) evergreen ground covers. It is excellent when used as a large-scale planting under trees, likes partial shade, and is usually weed-free.

Lily of the Valley (*Convallaria majalis*) A hardy and adaptable plant that covers the ground tightly enough to eliminate weeds. The plants die down in cold winters, but come back every spring with white or pink fragrant flowers. They will grow in deep shade.

Silveredge Goutweed (*Aegopodium Podagraria*) This plant grows about a foot (30.5 cm) tall in sun or shade, poor soil, or good loam. It is a vigorous grower, and can become a weed in good soil. In colder climates, the foliage dies to the ground in winter but comes back readily in the spring. It is drought-resistant.

Carpet Bugle (*Ajuga reptans*) One of the fastest-growing 6-inch (15-cm) ground covers, with spikes of blue flowers in the spring. It grows best in light shade; there are forms with variegated leaves. You should be warned that it is a favorite food and hiding place for slugs.

Other Possibilities

Spotted Dead Nettle (*Lamium maculatum*) This is one of the many plants that came over from Europe in ships' ballast and escaped to gardens. It belongs to the mint family, grows about 6 inches (15 cm) high in light shade, and crowds out weeds. In the past, John has found his nettle plants with some flowers still blooming and leaves still green on December 10!

Some of the plants from Europe get overlooked by the nursery trades here. This is one of the rapid growers and long bloomers that you should try. You may have difficulty finding this particular nettle at your favorite garden center, but some of your gardening friends will be glad to give you some cuttings or divisions.

Pulmonaria (*P. officinalis, P. saccharata*) Like many others, this plant has several common names, but is most often called "lungwort." It is one of the ground covers that often gets overlooked in colder climates and for growing in the shade. In the spring, it has pink flowers that fade to blue, and daintily splotched leaves. It makes a nice tight cover on the ground, usually crowding out weeds. We have both used *Pulmonaria*, and find it one of the best ground covers as long as you keep it out of the full sun of summer.

Ground Phlox (*P. subulata*) One of the delights of springtime is the 6-inch (15-cm) carpet of vivid white, pink, red, or blue provided by the newer varieties of ground phlox. It grows best in full sun.

Heather (*Erica sp.*) There are 500 species of this heather that are native to Europe and South Africa, some of which will grow in the milder climates of North America. The most useful is *Erica carnea*, which comes in several varieties — white, pink, purple, and deep red. From Scotland comes *Calluna vulgaris* in about

20 varieties — white, pink, purple, and crimson. From Ireland and northern Spain, we get *Daboecia cantabrica*, with white, pink, and purple flowers.

If you grow the heathers in an acid soil and in the sun, they will be among the most colorful of the care-free ground covers.

Crown Vetch (*Coronilla varia*) Riding along the highway, you have probably seen the banks covered with crown vetch, ranging in color from pale pink to lavender. The colonists probably brought this plant from Europe, and because of its deep rooting system, it has become one of our most useful ground covers for erosion control. You can sow seed, but you get better coverage if you plant plugs. The plant is drought-resistant, and one plug will cover an area 6 feet (1.8 m) in diameter.

Cotoneaster (*C. Dammeri*) This prostrate, rooting ever-green comes from China, and is a rapid grower, loaded with red berries in the fall. It grows best in light shade and needs a little pruning each fall.

Juniper (*Juniperus sp.*) The prostrate, evergreen junipers are among the best of the care-free ground covers for city conditions and dry soil. There are so many varieties that you should really visit a nursery and see them, in order to select what you like. One of the most popular is a cultivar called *tamariscifolia*. The junipers require as little attention as any of the ground covers.

One thing you do have to know is what the mature size of the individual juniper will be. You can put a nice little 2-foot (61-cm) wide plant in a space where it fits perfectly, and then be surprised to find that it grows to be 10 feet (3 m) wide. Ask your nurseryman about the mature size!

Barren Strawberry (*Waldsteinia fragarioides*) This is one of the lesser-known ground covers that we have found very satisfactory. Native to North America, it forms a tight mass with yellow flowers, and likes a soil rich in humus or compost.

Anemone (*A. blanda*) You don't usually think of members of the buttercup family as ground covers, but this is one from Greece. If you plant the tubers close together, you get a solid carpet of rich, sky blue in the spring. The flowers are almost 3 inches (7.5 cm) across and not over 6 inches (15 cm) tall. Trying plants like this makes working with ground covers fun.

SOME BACKGROUND ON PRIVACY

Centuries ago, when people in Europe, Egypt, and Japan desired privacy, they built walls, atriums, hedges, and screened enclosures. We have both been to Britain and driven down roads only 7 feet (2 m) wide defined by hedgerows about 6 feet (1.8 m) high on both sides. The British like their privacy, and the hedgerows certainly achieve it! When John was in Britain, he often tried to photograph a beautiful front garden by poking his camera over a high wall or hedge, and was frequently reminded by the residents that he was invading private property.

When the first colonists came from Europe, they found a large, expansive country where there was lots of room for gardens and little need to guard privacy.

The population was very sparse, and as they migrated west there were often hundreds of miles between neighbors.

The colonists gave up the enclosed front yard of Britain, and moved their gardens back against the foundation of the house. Since there was a need for the friendly presence of neighbors, the entire front of the property was often developed as a place to relate to other people.

Verandahs, porches, and porticos were the architectural component of this public, open approach designed to invite people in. We can both remember sitting in rocking chairs on front porches, holding conversations with people walking by on the street.

Because the early settlers spent so much time in their front yard, that is where the flower and herb gardens were carefully tended. Out front it was easier to show the garden to visitors or to talk about it while sitting on the porch.

In the 1920s a man who lived on the only street of a Maine town built his outhouse in the front yard. When seated, he left the top of the dutch door open so that he wouldn't miss chatting with his friends as they went by. This was neighborliness carried to the extreme!

In the 1990s, things are quite different, and we are beginning to understand why the front garden enclosure developed in Europe. As our population density increases, we are realizing that perhaps it is better to enclose the front garden for pollution, traffic, and noise control, as well as to have more space for gardens and to reduce street noise. You can accomplish all of these objectives by using the right enclosures.

FRONT YARD ENCLOSURES

To help you decide whether you want your front garden to be public or private, here are some ideas of what can be achieved by enclosing the front yard. The proper enclosures can make your front garden a much healthier and more pleasant place to live, and define a new area for your use. As subdivision lot sizes decrease, you will want to use all your property for yourself, rather than devote some of it to the pleasure of onlookers.

Privacy

The degree of privacy that is desired should be a consideration in the design of a good urban garden. If you live in an urban setting, you doubtless have young people playing games in the street or a steady stream of cars going by with the passengers able to see everything you are doing in the front yard. You can use the right enclosure to have whatever degree of privacy you wish, from the complete privacy of a 6-foot (1.8-m) brick wall to the partial privacy of a low barberry hedge.

Leib and Sheila Wolofsky live on a high-traffic road, and along the road edge of the property they have planted a hedge of forsythia that they do not prune. Unpruned, the forsythia grows to be about 12 feet (3.7 m) wide and almost as high, and acts as a screen and absorbs sound. It is a riot of yellow in the spring. This border enclosure shuts out all the disturbance of the adjacent road and allows the Wolofskys to have a back porch that is very private. Their yard is so quiet that even the cardinals come to the porch bird feeder.

Safety

Levels of crime and violence are reaching an all-time high in large urban centers, and not even small towns seem completely safe anymore. This makes us think of enclosing the front yard as a safety measure, to put a barrier between the family and the unpredictable element of the public out on the street. If you place colorful garden creations strategically, within a high-privacy safety enclosure, you'll be able to enjoy them from a window in the living room.

Noise Control

Every year the noise in our cities and urban areas increases and creates ill feeling and stress. Using plant barriers, you can absorb, deflect, reflect, or refract unpleasant sounds, from whatever source. Leafy trees break up the sound waves, scatter them in random directions, and reduce the decibels that reach the human ear. Even grass absorbs some of the sound waves passing over it.

If you live on a heavy-traffic street, you can reduce the noise in your front yard by several decibels if you plant a hedge of yew or cypress, at least 2 feet (61 cm) thick, at the front edge of your property.

Add a few trees to the front yard, and your home will be a much quieter place in which to live. We live in a fast-paced, noisy world, and although we probably can't slow it down, we can use plants to reduce the noise level at home and free ourselves from one source of stress.

The Living Wall

The willow wall is a living sound-barrier wall developed by Johann Aul, superintendent of parks in Hamburg, Germany. This wall is made of a double row of woven willow branches, with soil between the rows. The willow roots in the soil and creates a green hedge with excellent sound-absorption qualities. If street noise is a problem, this is an excellent solution. There are several other living sound-barrier walls in use in Europe; you might ask your landscape architect about them.

Hedges

Hedges are really living walls used to define space, just like the walls inside a house. When you are designing your own property, you should get acquainted with the many kinds of plants that you can use for hedges. One way to do this is to look at hedges as you drive around your own city. When you see one that you like, don't be timid! Knock on the front door of the house and ask for the name of the hedge plant and where it came from. You'll be surprised at how happy people are to help you!

Hedges are the ideal plants for screening off unsightly elements, such as factories or telephone poles, that can be seen from your garden. You will want a tall hedge so that you get the screening effect when you are standing up as well as sitting down. If you visit Schonbrunn Castle in Vienna, you will find sheared beech hedges 40 feet (12.2 m) tall that give a strong sense of shutting off the rest of the world.

Other Walls

You can use stone, brick, or concrete walls to define spaces. To absorb sound and soften the looks of such walls, we would suggest using vines to create a lacy green pattern and splashes of color. Just as loud sounds can be offensive to the ear, blank masonry walls can be offensive to the eye. Solid brick walls at least have a pattern, and fenestrated brick creates interesting light and shadow patterns. If you live where field stone is available, use it to make an attractive dry wall of colored limestone or slate.

Walls have defined the privacy of European families for hundreds of years. And inside, rigid lines of the walls are softened by gardens in atriums or courtyards, creating relaxed and graceful ambience.

Fences

One of the considerations in using enclosures is the question of space. If you have very limited space, a cedar fence with a width of only 4 inches (10 cm) might be a better choice than a hedge with a width of 3 feet (91 cm). You can always put vines on the fence for greenery.

There are new fences made of wrought iron, wood, and high-impact plastics, and there are advantages to each of them. The wrought-iron fence has less bulk, and allows filtered vision into the area it defines. Wooden fences can complement the architecture of the house, or can blend quite easily into the yard. For smaller areas, bamboo makes a pleasing, restful fence, and for larger areas, post and rail is still one of the best solutions. Fences using materials such as canvas or asbestos board as panels between the posts have a very sleek, modern appearance.

Before you add a new fence to your backyard garden, be sure to inquire at your city or town hall to see if there are ordinances concerning fences. It is also wise to check with telephone and utility offices before you dig post holes and find you have severed your phone or power line.

Gates

The type of gate that you use in a fence probably adds more to the architectural charm than the fence itself. Gates have had a prominent role throughout the history of gardening. One of the striking sights in St. Petersburg, Russia, is the number of artistic and ornate wrought-iron gates. Here is a chance to have the fun of designing your own gate, one that fits your particular situation. If you have a wooden fence, you can add design flair by choosing the right hardware for hinges and latches.

THE BACKYARD

In the backyard you can use enclosures to define the

vegetable garden and outdoor utility room from the living and recreation areas. To save space and add color, this is a good place for cedar fencing covered with climbing roses, clematis, or wisteria.

Microclimates

When you use an enclosure to define a space, you are creating new microclimates at the same time. It is a good idea to make a sketch of the backyard and then put up a little wind sock, so that you can record on the sketch the direction of the wind at different times of the year. An enclosure barrier can force cold winter winds up into the air and make a new, warmer microclimate within the enclosure. It is often the cold winter wind that freezes the early buds before they can bloom.

Purchase some inexpensive thermometers and post them on stakes around the backyard. Record temperatures daily for a couple of weeks. Then do the same thing after you put in an enclosure and see what a difference it makes in temperature control.

Plants alter adverse microclimates to make the environment healthier, by controlling both wind and temperature. Underneath a canopy of leafy trees, the temperature can be as much as 25°F (16°C) lower than above the canopy. When you plant evergreens against the wall of your house, you create a dead air space that helps to insulate the building and keep it warmer than a bare wall.

Air Drainage

Remember that cold air runs downhill like water, so if

your backyard slopes, the cold air will run to the lowest spot. You don't want to trap this cold air behind a solid board fence or a tight hedge. Your garden design should let the cold air flow off your property if possible.

Wind Chill

Many people forget the wind chill factor that is given on some weather reports. When the temperature is 0°F (–18°C) and the wind is blowing at 30 miles (48 km) per hour, the impact on people and plants is that of –49°F (–45°C). That's why it is dangerous. Even in milder conditions, when the temperature is 30°F (–1°C) and the wind is 30 miles (48 km) per hour, it feels like and can do as much damage as –2°F (–19°C). So using a fence or tight hedge enclosure can virtually eliminate the wind chill problem for a small area.

Traffic Control

One of the important uses of enclosures is to control the movement of people and animals. There are animals running free in almost any neighborhood, but one thing they will avoid is spiny hedge material. If you have bird feeding stations in your backyard, you are bound to have the local cats coming to visit and hoping to catch a nice feast of birds. You probably can't achieve complete control, but a hedge full of thorns will discourage predator cats.

Sometimes children living nearby find the shortest way to travel the neighborhood is across the corner of your lot. You will find that they don't like spiny and thorny hedge material either!

Pollution Control

All of the plant materials that you use for enclosure also have an engineering function, which is cleaning the air of pollen, bacteria, smoke particles, and dust from the street. Plants do this by washing the air. A mature beech tree will give off about 100 gallons (455 L) of water vapor into the air on a hot summer day. This water vapor attaches itself to the wind-borne air pollutants, and forces them to drop to the ground. Another source of water vapor is the moisture exuded through the leaves of some plants, a process called guttation.

The leaves of many plants are covered with very fine hairs, which trap the particulate pollutants in the air. The noxious gases in the air are actually taken into the leaves of plants, where they are chemically converted. For example, carbon dioxide is taken into the leaf, where the carbon is used to make plant tissue and oxygen is given off as a by-product.

The list of outdoor plants that absorb pollutant gases and clean the air gets longer every year. Even obnoxious odors can be controlled to some degree by plants. The more plant material you use for enclosures and screening, the cooler and cleaner the air on your property will be. You'll notice your health improving as well.

CHAPTER 9

DESIGNING FOR LIMITED PHYSICAL CONDITIONS

GARDENING MINISTERS TO THE NEEDS OF
THE SOUL WHICH SOMETIMES HUNGERS, THIRSTS AND
SHIVERS, WHILE THE BODY IS LUXURIOUSLY
FED AND CLOTHED IN FINE RAIMENT.
— *Frank M. Lupton,* Farmers and
Housekeepers Cyclopaedia, *1888*

When age brings changes to your physical condition, and you want to continue gardening, it is time to redesign your garden to suit your capabilities. In other words, practice good ergonomics. If you are ambulatory, you may need changes to solve problems with balance, coordination, or mobility, while gardening in a wheelchair will require smooth, wide pavement and raised beds, such as are found in a traditional courtyard. You should probably take some time to consider the surfaces in your garden area — how much should be lawn, how much pavement, and how much garden. If you are severely physically limited, for instance, you might want 75% in pavement, 25% in garden, and no lawn.

In this chapter we will discuss the kinds of changes that fit most types of limited physical abilities.

RAILINGS

Perhaps the mechanisms that control balance wear out as we age, for many of us find a cane helps us move about the garden more comfortably. For extra security you can add stout, strong railings to walks, ramps, and steps. You can use wrought iron, metal pipe, wood, or rope. The important thing is to have the railing posts set in enough concrete to make them sturdy. Set the posts in concrete 2 feet (61 cm) deep and about a foot (30.5 cm) in diameter. The posts

With the proper walkways and equipment, even people with restricted movement can continue gardening.

should be no more than 4 feet (1.2 m) apart for reliable support. When you feel off-balance, you can grasp the rail with your hands, or simply lean against it. In either case the railing must be strong enough to provide adequate support. The diameter of a round or oval rail should be sized for a small or crippled hand to grasp easily. If you use wood, be sure that it is finished, so that there is no danger of getting splinters in the hand.

Good railings make steps, ramps, and walks much easier to navigate, both indoors and out in the garden.

RESTING LOCATIONS
Limited-ability gardening is much easier if you can sit down and rest as frequently as you feel the need. This means having chairs, lounges, or benches placed wherever you need them in the garden. There is a great variety of garden seating equipment available, made of metal, wood, and plastic. Some of the most comfortable seating is the cushioned outdoor furniture marketed for use on the patio. In Chapter 2 we discussed the ergonomic equipment needed for gardening while sitting down.

By joining a garden club, you can perhaps help raise the money or exert the influence needed to get better limited-ability facilities in public gardens and parks.

SHADE
Ultra-violet radiation is currently increasing in many places around the world. Shade trees, gazebos, and

even garden umbrellas will provide shelter from the sun for older gardeners with sensitive skin.

WALKWAYS

The garden must be organized for traffic flow. If you use a walker and/or wheelchair, you may find your existing walkways are too narrow. A walkway for wheelchairs should be at least 4 feet (1.2 m) wide, and up to 6 feet (1.8 m) wide if you want to make it comfortable for two people to pass by each other. After you have located the walkways, select materials for paving that permit smooth, easy movement from one part of the garden to another. The following list of some of the available materials will help you make the right selection.

Brick

The charm of brick perhaps accounts for the fact that it has been used in walkways and terraces for hundreds of years. You get a warm, rich feeling from brick that you don't from other paving materials, and they can be laid in a variety of patterns to add interest.

If you plan to have brick laid on a concrete base and mortared in, then you should probably have it done by a professional. The secret is to make sure the brick is confined along the edges of the walkway, either with pressure-treated lumber or metal edging. As long as a brick walkway is well-confined, it will last for years and will provide an easy surface for gardeners with walking problems or those confined to wheelchairs.

Bricks come in several grades for different building purposes. For garden walkways, use severe-weather or concrete paving bricks. These are manufactured to withstand the freezing and thawing of colder areas.

Asphalt
We both feel that this is the least compatible surface to use for easy movement in the home garden. Because it holds the heat of the sun, melts at high temperatures, is drab black, and is there to stay, you should think twice before selecting asphalt. You don't want to be tracking black, sticky stuff into the house!

Concrete
So much of the concrete that we see in public places is so drab, dull, and monotonous that it seems a poor surfacing material for the garden. This type of concrete is used for the heavy traffic of many people. The light traffic of the garden lets you use the new patterned and colored finishes that make concrete look like many natural materials.

The common float finish gives you a smooth surface, but it may get coated with algae and be too slippery for the limited-ability gardener. A brush finish gives you a finely textured surface that is much safer for those who have walking problems. Wheelchairs roll over this surface easily. Exposed aggregate is a safe, natural-appearing finish, made by tamping small pebbles into the concrete before it has set up and become hard. It is not an easy surface to install and costs more than a brush finish.

There are companies that specialize in coloring and scoring concrete in attractive patterns that will fit any landscape setting. This finish gives good traction and adds interest. You can use precast concrete paving blocks, but we don't feel that they have any major advantages over patterned concrete poured at the site.

Like all paving surfaces, concrete is only as good as the base you put under it. A good base has total excavation of topsoil and vegetative matter, and a well-compacted stone or gravel layer for drainage. The surface must be even and sloped to avoid pockets of water, ice, and snow.

If the concrete is properly installed by a professional, you can avoid it being stained by salt or oil or having it crack. Concrete is one of the best walkway surfaces because it requires very little maintenance.

Flagstone
For richness and durability, no material equals natural flagstone. An amazing variety of slate, shale, sandstone, limestone, and marble is quarried across North America, and is available in a galaxy of colors for garden use.

Most of these natural flagstones require a skilled stonemason to shape and install them properly, and for this reason they are expensive. Flagstone installed on a concrete base with mortared joints makes an excellent pathway or walk.

Interlocking Paving
Interlocking cement paving blocks are currently very

popular for paths, driveways, and patios. They come in a variety of colors and shapes to create an attractive design surface, and are easy for people in walkers and wheelchairs to navigate.

These paving blocks originated in Germany at the time of World War II, to provide surfaces durable enough to support Leopard tanks. In more recent times, they have proved a popular choice for downtown streetscapes and home landscape surfaces. Some of their advantages are that they are frost-proof; they can be mass-produced; they are easily lifted and replaced for utility servicing or other renovations; they are manufactured to look like brick or cobblestone; and above all, they are relatively inexpensive.

The base for interlocking paving should have crushed stone about 6–8 inches (15–20 cm) deep with a 1-inch (2.5-cm) layer of fine stone screenings on top of this. After the paving blocks are laid, the surface should be brushed with masonry sand to fill the joints and then firmly pressed into place with a power compactor. A contractor should do the installation with the proper equipment, to provide an adequate surface for the limited-mobility gardener.

River Stone
For the non-traffic areas, river stone is one of the most interesting garden surfaces. Many Oriental gardens create a dramatic effect by using river stone to simulate water courses, or actually provide a bed for a small brook or garden stream. The stones vary in size, and are

rounded and well polished like the scree deposits you find in rivers.

You can use river stone as a zero maintenance surface under shrub beds, and for narrow strips next to a foundation where plant growth is difficult. The stones also make an excellent surface for rock gardens, as they reflect the conditions of alpine plants in their native habitat.

For low maintenance you should install river stone over a layer of black polyethylene sheeting, to prevent weed growth. A smooth layer of sand under the polyethylene will prevent tears or punctures.

RAISED BEDS

All flower beds can be converted to raised beds for easy access. You can do this with a variety of materials, including railroad ties, dimension lumber, concrete blocks, and vertical logs, but perhaps the best answer is to use interlocking stone made for retaining walls, steps, and planters. One advantage of this material is that the wall can be capped with a layer of stone wide enough to sit on comfortably.

In many instances, it will be advantageous to put a walk of interlocking paving stone around the raised bed. You need professional landscape help and equipment to install a first-class walk that will allow working on the bed from a wheelchair. The interlocking blocks for the walls of the raised bed are not as difficult to install, and with the help of a husky young high school student, you may be able to construct

Raised bed gardening is a good solution for wheelchair-bound gardeners.

your own. When you build the walls, be sure to recess the bottom layer of blocks so that you leave a toe space of at least 4 inches (10 cm) to make working on the bed easier (70, 89).

If a walkabout garden is not comfortable, you might put a raised bed at the edge of a patio, where it is easily accessible from a wheelchair or garden stool.

Height
The height of the bed depends upon the gardener.

There is an ergonomic height that fits the physical conditions of the user, so do some measuring and decide what height is best for you. Generally, the beds should be 24–30 inches (61–76 cm) high and about 3–4 feet (91–122 cm) wide. If you keep the planting beds narrow, people standing up won't have to lean in, and those in wheelchairs will be able to reach the back of the bed with long-handled tools. The length is just a matter of how much space you have available.

More of our botanical gardens are now displaying raised beds, to show people how they are constructed and to give the home owner a chance to see how such a planting area will fit his or her condition. Many hospitals and nursing homes are using raised beds for people with severe limitations on their ability to move freely. This is another place that is worth a phone call or a visit to get a better idea of how raised beds can make your gardening easier.

THEME GARDENS
Some of the seed companies are now marketing theme garden seed packets. You can have gardens specifically for low maintenance, patios, fragrance, cut flowers, and edible plants, each out of a package of seed. Each packet contains both seeds and plans for a suitable theme garden with the proper blend of height, time of bloom, and color coordination. These theme gardens are ideal for raised beds, where caring for the plants would be easy (28).

DECKS

Modern decks offer some attractive advantages for the gardener with limited physical ability. Many homes could add a deck at the same floor level as the house, to provide easy access and a chance for people with walkers or in wheelchairs to garden in containers, planting boxes, or even a greenhouse.

The ample supply of pressure-treated wood makes decks more practical than ever. A deck is no longer a square or rectangular platform adjoining the kitchen door. On level ground, a deck may stretch across the entire length of the house, with access from several rooms to provide outdoor gardening.

On steep slopes, you can have much more activity space with minimal disruption to your site. Broad safe stairways or ramps can provide linkage between decks or landings that have benches or seats in conversational settings. You might consider adding a deck to your front yard, to function much as the porch did in the past.

We recommend cedar, redwood, or pressure-treated pine and spruce lumber. New hardware simplifies and improves deck construction. Metal joist hangers make it easier for the do-it-yourself deck builder, and new metal clips fasten the planking down so that you have no exposed nail heads in the deck surface. Whatever the deck material, you should treat it with a water sealant.

RAMPS

In recent decades society has finally given recognition to those who are physically handicapped and whose mobility is limited to the wheelchair. You have noticed that it is now mandatory in public buildings to provide ramp access and easy-opening doorways. It is time to incorporate easy, gently sloped ramps into your garden.

The gardeners who find steps difficult should get from grade to grade with a ramp. Firm footing is the important consideration, and this means a poured-concrete or wooden ramp, installed by a landscape professional. For wheelchairs and walkers, the ramp should rise about 8 inches (20 cm) in 10 feet (3 m) of length and have a width of 3 feet (91 cm) and a gradient of 1:15. For a steep slope, the ramp can be divided into a series of switchbacks or hairpin turns, which will result in a longer, much easier path to climb.

DESIGNING A FRAGRANCE GARDEN FOR THE BLIND

Fragrance and gardens have long been associated. The earliest botanic gardens in Western civilization were herb gardens. Fragrant herbs, both culinary and medicinal, were a significant part of the medieval garden. Today most fragrance gardens are designed for the pleasure of the sightless. Quite often, the sense of smell becomes more acute when the other senses are diminished. The sense of smell is certainly more developed in some individuals than others — some say more so in the female than in the male sex. But even to the least discriminating of noses, well-known plants have a scent that is never forgotten after the first memorable exposure — a type of imprint on the brain.

We recommend that you consider the following when you are designing a fragrance garden: rose, lily of the valley, lilac, hyacinth, freesia, nicotine, gardenia, sweet clover, bayberry, lavender, juniper, eucalyptus, mint, scented geraniums, and balsam fir. Frangipani (*Plumeria*), also known as the Nosegay Tree because of its strong perfume, is also a potent choice.

Many plant fragrances are released intermittently, depending on the weather or time of day. Others, such as the scented geranium, yield fragrance only when you crush a leaf, and are a delight to the blind. Visit a garden for the blind and get ideas for the type of walkways and beds, as well as plants, that will provide pleasure for the sightless. We have not seen a garden for the blind with braille plant labels, but this might be helpful.

GARDEN DESIGN FOR THE PARTIALLY SIGHTED

The person with partial sight will enjoy a garden that has large-flowered, brightly colored plants. If these plants are placed so that they result in large masses of color, the partially sighted will get more pleasure than single plantings, spaced widely apart, can provide. Foliage that moves in the wind, like quaking aspen, is easier to see and soothing and musical to the ears. If you use labels for the plants, the lettering should be very large.

Recent research is showing that touch is very therapeutic. When a person with sight problems touches the velvety smooth leaf of the mullein plant, it elicits a different response than touching the rough, coarse foliage of the castor bean. The feel of soft firs and hemlocks contrasts with the prickly texture of spruce and some of the pines, while the large rough blossoms of a sunflower are dramatically different from the tiny flowers of coral bells. Use a variety of texture in both flowers and foliage to provide a rich touch experience.

MULCHING

When you apply material to the surface of the ground to reduce the need for weeding, to conserve moisture, and enrich the soil, this is called mulching. Nature was gardening successfully long before humans appeared on the planet, and we have only recently begun to take a closer look at what nature is doing. One of the best ways to make most of your garden area maintenance-free is to use mulch on all the garden beds.

If you walk into a woodland, you will find that all the leaves and needles fall to the ground and form a thick spongy layer of decaying vegetation, a mulch called "duff" by the foresters. This layer of duff helps regulate temperature by keeping the ground warm when the air is cold and protecting the soil from over-heating on hot sunny days. Earthworms like the moderate conditions under a mulch, and digest the decaying organic material to provide food for plants.

If your rose garden presently has more weeds than you enjoy pulling, you can virtually eliminate the weeding problem by applying the proper mulch. The existing weed seed in the ground may sprout under the mulch, but will die without access to the light of the sun. What a joy to be able to just pick the roses, instead of spending hours weeding!

This procedure, combining mulching and composting, has kept the forests of the world in prime growing condition for centuries, and it will do the same for the home garden. To help you begin using mulch, read an excellent overview of the subject (67).

Types of Mulch
There are many materials you can use for mulch, some organic and others inorganic. We both prefer to use the organic mulches, and for the average home owner this means grass clippings and leaves. There are all kinds of foil, asphalt paper, fiberglass, and plastic sheets marketed for mulching, but these are not the organic recycling materials that nature uses in the forest. Some cities are now composting garbage to make a good organic mulch material.

You have to be careful when using sawdust or straw as a mulch, because the decomposition bacteria require nitrogen, and they will steal it from nearby plants if there isn't enough in the soil. When we use sawdust as a mulch, we add fertilizer that provides 1 pound (0.5 kg) of nitrogen for every 100 pounds (45 kg) of sawdust.

Techniques
The secret to a successful mulch is to keep it thin, not

more than 3–4 inches (7.5–10 cm) when it is matted down. If the mulch is too thick, it will suffocate the roots of many plants. We both use grass clippings on our gardens, and in the fall, we collect the leaves with an electric vacuum that shreds the leaves and makes them suitable for mulch or compost.

A good way to water gardens that have a mulch cover is to place drip-irrigation tubes under the mulch so that all you have to do is turn on a faucet. For even less work, use a water timer on the faucet.

There is no doubt that one of the best ways to eliminate gardening strains and demands on the aging human body is to learn all you can about using mulches.

EASY INDOOR GARDENING
We discussed indoor gardening for the active senior in Chapter 5. In this chapter, we will consider changes for the limited-ability gardener living in an apartment or a nursing home.

Easy Watering
Many of us find it difficult to make several trips lugging watering cans between the kitchen sink and all the plants on the windowsills. We use an indoor watering hose that eliminates this problem. The hose is about ¼ inch (6 mm) in diameter, 60 feet (18 m) long, and comes on a reel. You fasten the hose to a kitchen faucet, turn the water on gently, and go water your plants. The brass nozzle has an on-off trigger valve on

a 2-foot (61-cm) wand, so you don't spill any water or carry any weight. When you are through watering, wind the hose up on the reel and store it on a kitchen shelf (27). This is one of the easiest devices for the wheelchair gardener to use.

Window Gardens
Instead of having plants scattered in several rooms, try bringing them together in a nice sunny, southern window garden. We use a table that is the same height as the windowsill, and that is about 4 feet (122 cm) long and 2 feet (61 cm) wide. The table is just high enough so that the arms of your wheelchair can go under its edge. There is no problem with washing the window, since the table is on casters and can easily be moved out of the way.

Terrariums
A terrarium is really a miniature greenhouse. We use a fish aquarium with a flat piece of glass for a top. Growing plants in this enclosed environment is easier than growing them in the open air, because both water and air are recycled inside the container. The water vapor given off by the plants condenses on the glass walls and runs back into the soil. During the day the plants give off oxygen and take in carbon dioxide. At night the plants burn up the carbon dioxide in the growth process, recycling the gases.

Growing plants in enclosed environments began in Greece about 500 B.C. In 1832, Dr. Nathaniel Ward discovered that he could successfully ship plants from England to Australia in terrariums, which were then called Wardian cases. Since then, indoor gardeners have learned that this is an effective way to grow some of the tender tropical species, avoiding the problems of dry air and drafts (49).

We have enjoyed growing Chinese evergreen (*Aglaonema comutatum*), miniature begonia (*Begonia boweri*), dwarf creeping fig (*Ficus pumila minima*), miniature gloxinia (*Sinningia pusilla*), bird's nest fern (*Aspenium nidus*), and many other plants in terrariums.

If you are just starting with terrarium growing, a good book will help (60).

Other stimulating indoor plant hobbies are forcing spring bulbs; cacti and dish gardening; flower arranging; starting your plants from seed, and growing carnivorous plants, miniature plants, aquatic plants, or one of the specialty plants that plant societies feature, such as African violets.

If you are fortunate enough to live in a metropolitan area, you will find that many botanical gardens, such as the one in Chicago, Illinois, provide opportunities for the seriously disadvantaged to gain hands-on gardening experience under the direction of skilled horticultural therapists. They have gardens with raised beds and all the special tools needed to facilitate limited-ability gardening.

PART FOUR

HORTICULTURAL THERAPY FOR THE LIMITED-ABILITY GARDENER

IN OUR LATER YEARS, MANY OF US EXPERIENCE CHANGES IN physical condition that severely limit our ability to garden. At this time, it might be a good idea to consider the services of a master horticultural therapist. Such a professional is trained to help you find the proper tools and equipment to continue gardening, in spite of handicaps.

CHAPTER 10

HORTICULTURAL THERAPY

I FARM THE SOIL THAT YIELDS MY FOOD.
I SHARE CREATION. KINGS CAN DO NO MORE!
— *Chinese gardener, 2500 B.C.*

Horticultural therapy is not a recent innovation — Egyptian physicians recommended walks in the garden for patients who were disturbed, and in the East the practitioners of Zen followed this course as well, even talking to plants. Roman women used lavender in their bathwater, and sachets and potpourri, oils, toilet water, and colognes in their daily beauty rituals.

The scope of horticultural therapy is tremendous. People of all ages, including those in retirement homes, nursing homes, hospitals, prisons, detoxifying clinics, and mental institutions, are benefiting from interaction with plants. Disturbed teenagers learn to control their temper and work off their aggressions by raking and hoeing, prisoners make baskets for sale to the public, the intellectually impaired learn to listen and follow directions, and have social interaction with staff, other patients, and volunteers. Horticultural therapy can enhance the quality of life for many different people.

When Maria Theresa was Empress of Austria, her

physician suggested that she should have a hobby for relaxation. She built a hobby greenhouse, two stories high and several hundred feet long, with a vast steel girder dome in its center. She then sent collectors all over the world to get unusual plants for her greenhouse.

HOSPITALS AND NURSING HOMES

As early as 1879, Friends Hospital in Philadelphia, Pennsylvania, had a greenhouse that was used as part of the treatment of mental illness. Today more than 300 hospitals in North America use horticulture as a therapy (70).

Many nursing homes offer horticultural therapy activities, either outside in raised beds, or in greenhouses that are accessible to wheelchairs. Others use workshops, and a few let the patients grow plants under lights in the wards.

Many of us don't realize that in Canada there are 300,000 people with Alzheimer's disease. At Homewood Health Centre in Guelph, Ontario, Mitchell Hewson, the horticultural therapist, has found that raising holiday plants helps restore the patients' sense of time; putting plants in a container, rooting cuttings, and pressing and drying flowers are activities which help the Alzheimer patient maintain a sense of reality and connection.

BOTANICAL GARDENS

Many of the more than 400 botanical gardens across North America provide facilities for horticultural therapy. The Royal Botanical Gardens in Hamilton, Ontario, has a teaching garden for all ages and all abilities. Brian Holley, the director, says that when disadvantaged people plant seeds and are rewarded with a harvest of food they can eat, it increases their self-confidence and gives them a sense of pride.

UNIVERSITIES

Many universities now have interdisciplinary research teams involving a dozen or more different branches of science. These research teams are studying the ways in which plants affect people. Their goal is to produce tested experimental data about how to use horticulture to improve the lives of individuals, communities, and nations. The horticulture industries are supporting this research into non-traditional areas to make sure that they are providing the best plants, products, and services to enhance human well-being.

In the past, keen minds have instinctively sensed the health value of gardens, trees, and flowers, in both the natural and urban setting. Now scientific research is beginning to validate their beliefs.

If gardening can help people with severe limitations, then it can certainly benefit those of us who are still gardening at an advanced age, with only minor aches and pains.

HORTICULTURAL THERAPY OUTREACH

Some botanical gardens have realized that many people find it difficult to get to their facilities, so they have established outreach programs that take the therapy facilities to the user. The Royal Botanical Gardens in Hamilton, Ontario, pioneered such a program over a decade ago, when their horticulturist, the late Ray Halward, solicited donations to put a "traveling greenhouse" on the road. This was a large van converted to a greenhouse with lights and benches, and well stocked with seeds, plants, soil, fertilizer, and heating equipment. With this unit Halward traveled to nursing homes, children's hospitals, and other institutions, to encourage and teach the disadvantaged how to grow and care for plants. A tragic twist of fate occurred when Ray's career ended with Alzheimer's disease. His activities enriched the lives of thousands during his very active years.

Check to see if there is a botanical garden anywhere near you that provides a similar service.

THE THERAPEUTIC BENEFITS OF GARDENING

Plants stimulate all the senses. Caring for them can bring back some of the emotions that many of us felt when raising our own children. There is a sense in which we are all children of the earth — plants *and* humans. Our experiences with plants can foster a feeling of connection to the earth.

Emotional

Many retired seniors find that time becomes an enemy and the days seem empty and without purpose. As we age, our self-image changes and we are likely to think less of ourselves than we did at the height of our career. Our self-image involves movement, feeling, and thought, and when any one of these components is neglected or restricted, we are likely to feel depressed. Gardening requires us to use all three elements of our self-image. Participating in the life process is a creative effort that serves to relieve boredom, anxiety, and stress. Caring for plants just makes you feel better.

People have a subliminal affinity for plants, and use them from the cradle to the grave in all the important rituals. There is now a treatment technique called phytopsychotherapy, which uses plants to help people with psychiatric disorders. We have both found that people who stay indoors in nursing homes are delighted with the fragrance of narcissus in a bowl or the striking size and color of amaryllis as it converts the energy stored in the bulb into vivid flowers. In the spring, you can take branches of forsythia or cherry to shut-ins, so that they can experience the change of seasons as the flowers open. Other suitable choices are flowering quince, pussy willow, magnolia, witch hazel, flowering almond, dogwood, and apple.

About 60,000 years ago, Neanderthal man had a sense of the emotional and spiritual content of plants, and sprinkled flowers over the corpse at the burial ceremony. As man came out of the forest into settlements, he brought the feelings of the forest with him in his garden. We are descended from humans who lived intimately with plants, using them for food, shelter, and medicine, and from them we inherited a sense of connection with nature. We express love with flowers on Valentine's Day and celebration with the poinsettia at Christmas, and use plants or flowers to cheer the sick or shut-in.

Physical

As we grow older, gardening gives us the right amount of exercise to improve the functions of the heart, blood vessels, lungs, muscles, and joints, as well as helping us keep our agility, mobility, and flexibility. Research at Rutgers University in New Jersey shows that blood pressure falls, muscles loosen, and heart rate slows while gardening, and this increases the body's resistance to stress. At the same time, gardening provides chemical-free food for better nutrition.

Even being near a green area can have beneficial effects. Robert Ulrich of the Texas A&M School of Architecture has found that people looking out a window at a grove of trees had lower blood pressure, more alpha-wave activity, and less muscle tension; required less in the way of painkillers; and recovered sooner than those viewing urban buildings.

Mental

One of the intangible benefits of gardening is the way that it influences the mind and the whole physiological system. Exercise for the mind is as important as exercise for the body. We both have friends who have stopped reading and don't watch informative TV programs; their very limited conversation is chiefly about the past. They seem to have decided that they are ready to pass on.

Gardening keeps the mind busy! You have to read seed catalogs, follow directions on boxes and bottles, understand how plants operate, and keep track of the proper time to do things. In order to be successful at gardening, you need even more information. This involves reading books, magazines, newspapers, and garden center information sheets. You should start listening to the garden programs on radio or watching them on TV. You can also buy your own videotapes and computer software to get gardening assistance. There is no time to get depressed when you have a garden.

Social
The social benefits of gardening are so important and widespread that we devoted a whole chapter (Chapter 6) to them!

Spiritual
The natural landscape of North America has long provided the urban dweller with spiritual uplift and renewal — think of visits to the great forests and alpine meadows of western North America, or the many lakes, waterways, and woodlands from California to Newfoundland. In other cultures and locations, nature also displays a variety of rich landscapes that can provide solace. From the moors of Scotland and the birch meadows of Sweden across Asia to

China, the gardens of nature can give people a sense of spirituality.

Gardens have reflected the spiritual beliefs and feelings of the people of many cultures. In China, both Taoism and Buddhism influenced the way gardens were designed and developed, so that the garden was a sacred place. The Oriental garden was made up primarily of native plants, sand, and rocks, without any great splashes of color. In fact, the Zen gardens were raked sand and rock with no plants at all. The Chinese spiritual sense was nature-based, and their gardens were small cross-sections of the grandeur, mystery, order, and peace of the natural world around them.

Plants are frequently used in Western religious celebrations. We all associate the white lily and palm leaves with the celebration of Easter, and over the last hundred years, the poinsettia has become the leading floral symbol for Christmas. The use of flowers for weddings and funerals indicates that there must be spiritual content associated with flowers. Many religions also set aside certain Sundays to celebrate the bounty of the plant world, such as Thanksgiving, when the church is decorated with cornstalks, pumpkins, and the fruits of the harvest.

Consider all the poetry that has been written about the spiritual impact of gardens and plants. Poets from Shakespeare to Wordsworth to Whitman have all tapped into their feelings about nature and plants. Poetry survives because it often expresses the same feelings that we have. One of our favorites is Joyce

Kilmer's poem "Trees."

APPRECIATING TREES

We tend to take trees for granted and forget that they are perhaps the single most important item in our landscape, giving us a comforting feeling of longevity, providing shade, and cleaning the air of pollutants. The sound of wind moving through trees is soothing and relaxing, and the canopy overhead gives us a feeling of being protected. When you walk into a grove of redwoods, you get the same spiritual feeling as when walking into a Gothic cathedral.

Many of the world's great religions have used trees as symbols of man's spiritual relation with the divine. In hundreds of European and British cathedrals, there are prominent carvings of "The Green Man," a human head with foliage for ears and face. The use of this figure in religious or spiritual ceremonies and rituals, particularly those of the Celts, goes back to remote antiquity, and indicates that we have a subliminal awareness of our dependence upon and relation to plants and trees.

When looking for trees for a landscape development, we found a man here on the Niagara Parkway who, years ago, bought 120 acres (48.6 hectares) of land on the banks of the Niagara River. Over a 40-year period he has planted 85,000 trees on the property. There are many examples of this type of dedication, all over the world, but the media seem to tell us only about trees destroyed — not trees planted.

When Sir Edmund Hillary was in the Himalayas,

he met a young Sherpa who was disturbed by the loss of trees on the upper slopes; they had been cut for firewood. He asked Hillary where he could go to learn how to reforest his homeland and Hillary suggested the University of Alberta. The young Sherpa went there, obtained his degree in forestry, and went back to begin a program of planting out seedlings of the proper species for the upper Himalayas.

Richard St. Barbe-Baker probably planted more trees than anyone who has ever lived. He was a professional forester who worked in North America, New Zealand, and Africa, where he was involved in planting 26 *trillion* trees.

Maybe we are beginning to appreciate trees! There are cities in Europe now where you are not allowed to cut down a tree, either on private or public property, without a permit. And think of the part trees play in our lives. How many parents have built a tree house for their children? We use trees to celebrate notable events. Switzerland has a tradition of planting a tree at the birth of a child — an apple for a boy and a pear for a girl. In Britain, there are groves where famous people have donated a tree; you can enjoy looking up at the broad spread of a tree donated by Queen Victoria. In North America some cemeteries use trees rather than grave markers or monuments to commemorate people.

In a recent editorial in *Harrowsmith Country Life*, John Barstow said, "Trees make comforting symbols because they live long enough but not forever (eternity frightens me). A pair of old rock maples by a long-deserted cellar hole connect me to a specific past, to the people four generations before me who planted the trees and attached to them their hopes. And yet planting a tree, if one chooses the site properly, can give one an anonymous sort of immortality." Recent research suggests that some of the bristlecone pines in California are as much as 11,000 years old, rather than only 5000. No matter what their age, when you stand and look at one of these gnarled old specimens, feelings of respect and admiration flow.

AROMATHERAPY

The history of fragrance is part of the history of civilization. Man has always enjoyed plants with pleasant aromas. Frankincense and myrrh were used in incense and perfume in biblical times and were equal in value to gold. In 1482 B.C. the Queen of Egypt sent collectors to Somaliland to bring back frankincense trees for her temple garden. Incense was introduced into the public worship of the Roman Catholic Church in the sixth century. The word "perfume" comes from the Latin *per fumum*, which means "through smoke." Since those early days, we have enjoyed plant fragrance, but are only now beginning to investigate the therapeutic properties of plant aromas.

Aromatherapy Research

When you walk into a pine forest, the air is refreshing. This is probably due to the molecules given off by the trees, although it may be that the pine air is free of smog and pollutants that create stress when we inhale normal city air. According to Dr. Gary Schwartz of the University of Arizona, when we breathe polluted air on the city street or in some of our poorly ventilated buildings, the aroma goes directly from the nose to the limbic center of the brain (the part that perceives odors) to make us feel tense and uncomfortable. Current research by Dr. Charles Wysocki, at the Monell Chemical Senses Center in Philadelphia, indicates that the limbic system is connected to many parts of the brain and is apparently responsible for emotional reactions such as mood changes.

The activity level of the cortex, and the whole body response, is influenced by what goes into the limbic system. Many plants release volatile, therapeutic oils from their leaves, flowers, and roots. Some of these oils have anti-bacterial properties. Scents such as lily of the valley or peppermint circulated in the air-conditioning system will improve work performance, according to University of Cincinnati research undertaken by Dr. William Dember and Dr. Joel Warm.

In Japan business firms are using lavender, jasmine, and lemon in environment fragrance systems with excellent results. Junichi Yagi at the Technology Center of America in Boston, Massachusetts, classifies some of the aromas as follows:

Relaxing: lavender and chamomile
Stimulating: jasmine and lemon

Invigorating: pine and eucalyptus
Anxiety Relief: heliotrope

We are even sensitive to aromas when we are
asleep, as is shown by the experiments of Dr. Peter
Badia of Bowling Green State University in Ohio. Dr.
Badia didn't find any aroma that fostered sleep, in
fact most plant fragrances disturbed sleep. So don't
place fragrant plants in the bedroom or outside the
bedroom window.

One way to describe the results of aromatherapy
research is simply to state that many plant aromas can
lift your spirits, and this is sufficient reason for having
a rose garden or a potted gardenia in the living room.
Stepping into a home greenhouse in midwinter to
smell the sweet peas can be a soothing delight, and can
alleviate depression.

Aromatherapy is widely practiced in England,
Germany, France, and Switzerland, but we need a lot
more research on the role that aromas play in the lives
of humans. (We do know that if you take a gardenia to
a patient in the hospital, all the ambulatory patients
drop in for a visit to share the fragrance.)

Medical Aromatherapy

Practitioners of holistic medicine are now using aromatherapy in their treatments. We visited an aroma-
therapist who is formulating a stress relief mixture for
anxious executives to inhale. She uses such scents as
peppermint, pine, and jasmine. When the pressure

builds, it is easy to take a little bottle out of your desk, put a dab of fragrance on the back of your hand, and enjoy the relaxation that aromatherapy brings.

Using Aromatherapy at Home
Many plants retain an aroma when dried, and there are literally hundreds of indoor and outdoor plants you can grow at home and use for potpourris. John grew up sleeping on a fir balsam pillow every night and even today is greatly refreshed by the aroma of fir.

If you want to enjoy aromatherapy in your car, you can buy a device that plugs into the cigarette lighter and wafts the fragrance of peppermint, juniper, rosemary, or basil through the air. These fragrances will also sometimes keep you more alert and aware while driving.

If you fly a lot, you might like to try alleviating the symptoms of jet lag with an aroma formulation called "After-Flight Regulator." It was developed in Britain and is available from Fragrant Offering Imports in Richmond, British Columbia.

Enfleurage is the process of making your own flower oils by mixing flower petals with odorless fats or oils. To make an ounce (28 mL) of rose oil essence may take as much as a ton (1000 kg) of rose petals, but daily sniffing in your own fragrant rose garden uses no petals!

For your own experience, try getting some small vials of various scents and see what reaction you have to different scents. To get the full effect of aromas such as jasmine, you really should have a hanging basket in full bloom in the house or greenhouse.

Aromatherapy Training
If you are intrigued by the prospects of aromatherapy, and would like to get more information or training, we suggest that you contact the Tisserand Institute. This institute offers a six-month diploma course, seminars, wall charts, and a complete mail-order service (47).

Aroma in Nature
All animals throughout the world have distinct odors, including humans, who spend a lot of money trying to get rid of their natural aroma. This was not the case in earlier times. Napoleon once wrote a letter to Josephine asking her not to wash because he was coming home shortly, which was an acceptable request at the time. Now we consider body odor to be objectionable, and scrub ourselves clean in order to put on the scents of other animals and plants that we consider to be more pleasant.

Our sense of smell is not as well developed as that of animals and insects. A German shepherd has about 220 million sensory cells in its nose. This permits the dog to recognize the unique scent of each human being and even to track one of a pair of identical twins. The male silkworm moth has 40,000 sensory cells on its antennae with which it can detect the mating odor of the female, 7 miles (11 km) away. With about 5 million sensory cells in the human nose, we are not able to perform such remarkable feats but we do find plant aromas enjoyable and soothing (74, 75).

We are not usually aware of the role aromas play in nature. When your cat rubs his cheek against your leg, he is depositing a scent from glands in his cheek to establish ownership. Mosquitoes are attracted to humans by the odor of the carbon dioxide we exhale.

EATING FLOWERS

More gardeners are becoming acquainted with food from the flower garden. There is a surprising variety of flower food, especially for salads and soups. Some California supermarkets even have pansy, tulip, and gladiolus petals for sale in the produce department. For further information, see *The Avant Gardener*, June 1992 (67), which includes an excellent bibliography. A word of caution — all flowers are not edible. As with mushrooms, you need to know what you are doing!

ALLELOPATHY

Many kinds of plants volatilize chemical scents from their leaves into the air and from their roots into the soil in a process called allelopathy. Some trees give off a chemical into the air when they are attacked by insects; the neighboring trees respond by producing more tannin in their leaves to be resistant to insect attack.

Other trees give off chemicals that are injurious to humans. We had an artist friend who built a house on the shore of Puget Sound in a grove of large-leaved maples. The prevailing wind came in from the west through the grove of maples and bathed the house in chemicals. Our friend developed a rash on her arms, and as a result had to sell the house and move to another location.

Continued research in aromatherapy will give us a better understanding of the role aroma plays in maintaining our health.

COLOR

Nearly all cultures have had gardens, from the hydroponic Hanging Gardens of Babylon to the floating island gardens of the Incas and Aztecs. Britain and Europe developed the use of color in foliage plants with carpet bedding in geometric designs. North America really brought the language of color to the garden with the introduction of hundreds of varieties of bedding plants. Mass plantings with great swatches of color are now common in our parks and home gardens.

Every spring, flower shows arrive to help us see some color, and get away from the flat tones of winter. In the summer, there is an annual holiday exodus from the city to visit the carpets of color in rural and alpine meadows. In the fall, you can tour the northern areas to admire the lavish display of rich golden yellow, scarlet, and burnished brown pigments that nature stores under the green chlorophyll in leaves.

Gardening lets us have the same riot of colors right at home in the yard. A good gardening pastime is to go through the seed catalogs, searching out flower colors for a succession of bloom right through the year.

Color permeates our lives in our painted structures, our decorating, food coloring, clothing, and the hair dyes and cosmetics on our bodies. Plants are the original chemical formulators and secrete over 2000 different pigments. Early tribal man used plant dyes principally for personal adornment.

Plant Dyes

The best **blue** dyes come from the leaves of indigo, a shrubby perennial that is now grown in India, Asia, and the East Indies. Synthetic indigo is not as permanent as the dye from plants. In some places in the world, such as Tajikistan, the plant dye is still used in textiles.

One of the best **red** dyes comes from a tropical tree introduced into Europe, where it was called "bresel" wood. When the Portuguese found a similar tree in South America, they called it "bresel," which became the name of the country, Brazil. The red color in the British army redcoat uniform was from cochineal, which comes from the dried bodies of a scale insect that feeds on *Ficus religiosa* in Mexico.

The Osage orange tree gave the American Indians the **yellow and gold** dyes often used in their war paints.

The **green** chlorophyll in leaves is extracted for use as a dye.

A brilliant **orange** dye comes from henna, a small tree native to the Mediterranean region. This dye has been used for fabrics, human hair, eyebrows, and fingernails.

The best **black** dye, which was used for ink, comes from a tropical tree called logwood. Before synthetic chemicals were produced, annual production of this dye was as much as 40,000 tons (over 40 million kg).

We inherited our sense of color from generations of ancestors who had only plant dyes available. Over the years, wild flowers have been domesticated, and we are able to see the colors of the plant world right at home in the garden.

PROFESSIONAL HORTICULTURAL THERAPY

There are three levels of professional expertise, horticultural therapist, horticultural therapy technician, and Master's horticultural therapist. See Chapter 1 for more information.

GERIATRICS AND GERONTOLOGY

The medical science dealing with the diseases, debilities, and care of the aged is known as geriatrics. The emphasis is on the medical aspects of aging. If you are interested in more information about geriatrics, the sources listed under books on ergonomic and horticultural therapy usually answer inquiries free-of-charge.

Gerontology is the study of the aging process, with emphasis on the special problems and needs of the aged. For more information, try one of the sources listed, which are just a sample of the many organizations that provide information and services for the elderly.

EPILOGUE

WE CAN THINK OF NO BETTER WAY TO CONCLUDE THIS
book than to give you the insights of a person who has
been exploring the people/plant relationship for many
years and is actively doing the current research.
Charles A. Lewis received the Arthur Hoyt Scott
Award for his contributions to horticulture in 1992
and inspired a very active researcher, Dr. Diane Relf, to
reflect as follows:

> Horticulture has played a role in all aspects of
> human culture. Plants have influenced our
> language, art, and literature. The art and
> science of cultivating plants changed civiliza-
> tion, and the search for plants guided early
> exploration. Human interaction in communi-
> ties is altered by the plants in the environ-
> ment. Community gardens, neighborhood
> plantings, and school gardens all bring
> people together, leading to continued interac-
> tion. Plants contribute to community pride
> and present a cost-effective way of improving
> a depressed urban area.
>
> Plants influence human behavior, physical
> health, and perceptions. Plants in defined

spaces present a microcosm of the natural environment, remove toxins and pollutants from the air, provide noise abatement, and reduce the harshness of constructed environments. Research indicates an effect of viewing vegetation on emotional states, cognitive functioning, physiological activity, and health-related indicators, including the fostering of recovery from stress and mental fatigue. Horticultural therapy is the specific application in the treatment of individuals with diagnosed problems and is becoming increasingly important.

Despite the intuitive sense of the importance of plants to human well-being, there is little documentation of its impact. Not until there is documented, credible evidence of the role of horticulture in human well-being will horticulture be given a high level of priority in public and private allocation decisions. The horticulture community must work together to quantify the impact of horticulture and make this resource available to a wide population.

SOURCES

FOR GARDEN PRODUCTS, INFORMATION, AND SEED

Both of us like to shop for garden equipment in places where we can see and handle the merchandise, but there are many garden products that are available only by mail order from garden supply companies, seed companies, and garden magazine advertising. We have collected a wide variety of current seed catalogs and magazines and find that many of them have extensive sections listing garden merchandise. You can have a lot of winter fun collecting some of these and sharing them with your gardening friends.

The following list is only a few of the many mail order sources, since we cannot list every garden center or nursery. We suggest that you collect your own catalogs to get acquainted with what the various centers offer.

A good place to start is with *Gardening by Mail* by Barbara Barton, which lists approximately 250 sources of products in Canada, the United States, and Britain. Don't forget the Yellow Pages for the garden centers nearest you!

SOCIETIES

1. American Association of Retired Persons, 601 E Street N.W., Washington, D.C. 20049. Publishes a periodical, *Modern Maturity*, full of information for seniors. There are 32 million members, and membership includes a subscription to the magazine.
2. The American Community Gardening Association, 325 Walnut St., Philadelphia, Pennsylvania 19106.
3. American Geriatrics Society, Boston University Medical Center, 75 East Newton Street, Boston, Massachusetts 02118. Tel.: 617-247-5019.
4. American Horticultural Society, River Farm, 7139 Boulevard Drive, Alexandria, Virginia 22308. Tel.: 800-777-7931. Excellent information a phone call away.
5. American Horticultural Therapy Association, 9220 Wightman Road, Suite 300, Gaithersburg, Maryland 20879. Tel.: 301-948-3010.
6. The American Society of Landscape Architects, 4401 Connecticut Avenue, Washington, D.C. 20008.
7. Canadian Association of Retired Persons, 27 Queen Street East, Suite 1304, Toronto, Ontario M5C 2M6. Publishes a quarterly newspaper.
8. Canadian Geriatrics Research Society, 351 Christie Street, Toronto, Ontario M6G 3C3. Tel.: 416-537-6000. Reference and consulting services.
9. Canadian Horticultural Therapy Association, c/o Royal Botanical Gardens, Hamilton, Ontario L8N 3H8. Tel.: 416-529-7618.
10. Canadian Hydroponics Ltd., 8318 120th Street, Surrey, British Columbia V3W 3N4.

11. Canadian Society of Landscape Architects, P.O. Box 870, Station B, Ottawa, Ontario K1P 5P9.

12. Disabled Independent Gardeners Association, 1632 Sutherland Avenue, North Vancouver, British Columbia V7L 4B7.

13. Feldenkreis Foundation, Box 70157 Washington, D.C. 20088. Tel.: 301-656-1548.

14. The Garden Council, 500 North Michigan Avenue, Suite 1400, Chicago, Illinois 60611. Tel.: 312-661-1700; Fax: 312-661-0769.

15. The Garden Tourist Press, 290 West End Avenue, New York, New York 10023.

16. Gerontological Information Center, University of Southern California, University Park, Los Angeles, California 90098. Tel.: 213-743-5990. Information on life-span development and aging. Answers inquiries and service is free.

17. Horticultural Therapy Society of England, Goulds Ground, Vallis Way, Frome, Somerset BA11 3DW.

18. Hydroponic Society of America, #218 2819 Crow Canyon Road, San Ramon, California 94583. Tel.: 510-743-9605.

19. IAMAT, 40 Regal Road, Guelph, Ontario N1K 1B5. Tel.: 519-836-0102, or 917 Center Street, Lewiston, New York 14092. Tel.: 716-754-4883.

20. The Indoor Light Gardening Society of America, c/o New York Horticultural Society, 128 West 58th Street, New York, New York 10019.

21. International Society of Arboriculture, 303 W. University St., Urbana, Illinois 61801. Tree care pamphlets.

22. National Geriatrics Society, 212 West Wisconsin Avenue, Milwaukee, Wisconsin 53203. Tel.: 414-272-4130. Care of geriatric patients in nursing homes.
23. People-Plant Council. Attn.: Dr. Diane Relf, Department of Horticulture, Virginia Polytechnic Institute and State University, Blacksburg, Virginia 24061-0327. Tel.: 703-231-6254.
24. Self-Help for the Elderly, 640 Pine Street, San Francisco, California 94108. Tel.: 415-982-9171. Services for the elderly. Inquiries answered free.

PRODUCT SOURCES

Recently there has been an explosion of garden products on the market. Manufacturers are marketing items that make the garden more beautiful and the gardening easier. If you go to the library and look through some of the garden magazines, you will get a peek at some of the thousands of new products that are available.

25. Applied Hydroponics, 3531 Kerner Boulevard, San Rafael, California 94901. Tel.: 800-634-9999.
26. Berry Hill Ltd., 75 Burwell Road, St. Thomas, Ontario N5P 3R5. Excellent flower towers.
27. Charley's Greenhouse Supplies, 1569 Memorial Hwy., Mount Vernon, Washington 98273. Tel.: 800-322-4707.
28. Dominion Seed House, Box 2500, Georgetown, Ontario L7G 5Z6. Tel.: 416-873-3037, 800-463-6944; Fax: 416-564-8038.

29. Equipment Consultants and Sales, 2241 Dunwin Drive, Mississauga, Ontario L5L 1A3. Tel.: 416-828-5925.

30. FMCI Hydroponics, 2402 Edith Ave., Burlington, Ontario L7R 1N8. Tel.: 416-333-3282; Fax: 416-634-9095. One of many!

31. Gardener's Eden, Box 7307, San Francisco, California 94120-7307. Tel.: 800-822-9600; Fax: 415-421-5153.

32. Gardener's Supply Co., 129 Intervale Road, Burlington, Vermont 06401. Tel.: 800-863-1700; Fax: 802-660-4600.

33. Hydrofarm Gardening Products, Pennsylvania (tel.: 800-227-4586), Ohio (tel.: 800-833-6868), Oklahoma (tel.: 800-356-3771), California (tel.: 800-634-9999).

34. Lee Valley Tools Ltd., Box 6295, Station J, Ottawa, Ontario K2A 1T4. Tel.: 613-596-0350; Fax: 613-596-6030.

35. Lifestyle Fascinations Inc., 12 Progress Place, Jackson, New Jersey 08527-2003. Tel: 908-928-1800; Fax: 908-929-1107.

36. Limestone Trail Co., 853 Lakeshore Road, Niagara-on-the-Lake, Ontario. Tel.: 416-646-7545; Fax: 416-646-7916. Great variety of gazebos and outbuildings.

37. McFayden Seeds, 30 9th Street, Box 1800, Brandon, Manitoba R7A 6N4. Tel.: 204-726-0759; Fax: 204-725-1888.

38. Mellinger's, 2350 West South Range Road, North Lima, Ohio 44452-9731. Tel.: 216-549-9861; Fax: 216-549-3716.

39. Paradise Water Gardens, 14 May St., Whitman, Massachusetts 02382. Supplies for and books on water gardening.
40. Smith and Hawken, 25 Corte Madera, Mill Valley, California 94941. Tel.: 415-383-2000; Fax: 415-383-7030.
41. SoilMoist JRM Chemical, 13600 Broadway Ave., Cleveland, Ohio 44125. Tel.: 800-962-4010.
42. Solar Components Inc., 121 Valley St., Manchester, New Hampshire 03103. Tel.: 603-688-8186: Fax: 603-672-3110. A 63-page catalog of everything solar!
43. Stokes Seed Co., 39 James St., Box 10, St. Catharines, Ontario L2R 6R6; or 1152 Stokes Bldg., P.O. Box 548, Buffalo, New York 14240. Tel.: 416-688-4300; Fax: 416-684-8411.
44. Swisher Mower Company, Box 67, Warrensburg, Missouri 64093. Tel.: 800-222-8183. Solar composters.
45. Terra-Sorb International, Box 10834, Bradenton, Florida 34282-0834. Tel.: 800-227-6728.
46. Tetrapond, 201 Tabor Road, Morris Plains, New Jersey 07950. Complete water garden supplies.
47. Tisserand Institute, 65 Church Road, Hove, East Sussex, England BN3 2BD. Tel.: 0273-206640.
48. The Toro Company, 8111 Lyndale Avenue, S. Minneapolis, Minnesota 55420. Tel.: 800-327-8676.
49. Vintage Gardening Accessories, 25 Charles St., Hingham, Massachusetts, 02043. Tel.: 617-740-1811.
50. Walt Nicke Co., 36 Mcleod Lane, Box 433, Topsfield, Massachusetts 01983. Tel.: 508-887-3388.

BIBLIOGRAPHY

BOOKS ON ADAPTIVE GARDEN DESIGN

Adaptive garden design is a relatively new field, with an emphasis on using ergonomics to help fit the garden to the gardener. As yet, the literature is not very extensive. With Chapter 1 as a background, we are listing what we have found as the best sources.

51. Bander, Robert G. *Landscaping and Garden Remodeling*. Menlo Park, California: Lane Publishing Co., 1990.
52. Barton, Barbara J. *Gardening by Mail*. Boston, Massachusetts: Houghton Mifflin Co., 1990. An enormous source book!
53. Brookes, John. *The Small Garden*. London, England: Tiger Books International, 1989.
54. ———. *The Book of Garden Design*. New York, New York: Macmillan Publishing Co., 1991. The best book currently available on garden design.
55. Burnetti, Marianne. *Tips for Carefree Landscapes*. Pownal, Vermont: Storey Communications, 1990.
56. Clark, David E. *New Western Garden Book*. Menlo Park, California: Lane Publishing Co., 1979.

57. Drysdale, Art C. *Gardening Off the Ground*. Toronto, Ontario: J.M. Dent & Sons, 1975. Worth checking out of the library!

58. Ernst, Ruth Shaw. *The Moveable Garden*. Chester, Connecticut: Globe Pequot Press, 1991.

59. Foster, Gordon F. *Ferns to Know and Grow*. New York, New York: Hawthorne Books, 1971.

60. Halpin, Anne M. *Encyclopedia of Indoor Gardening*. Emmaus, Pennsylvania: Rodale Press, 1980.

61. Harris, Marjorie. *Ecological Gardening*. Toronto, Ontario: Random House of Canada Ltd., 1991.

62. Horton, Alvin. *Gardening in Containers*. San Francisco, California: Ortho Books, 1984. Ortho publishes a long list of garden books; you can usually find them at your favorite garden center.

63. Jackson, Albert, and David Day. *Outdoors and Gardens*. New York, New York: Hearst Books, 1989. Excellent source for construction materials and methods. Good "how to" illustrations.

64. Kenyon, Stewart. *Hydroponics for the Home Gardener*. 2d ed. Toronto, Ontario: Key Porter Books, 1992.

65. Loxton, Howard. *The Garden, A Celebration*. Hauppage, New York: Barron's Educational Inc., 1991. The cream of coffee table books for the gardener.

66. Pierce, John H. *Home Solar Gardening*. 2d ed. Toronto, Ontario: Key Porter Books, 1992. Let the sun heat your house and greenhouse.

67. Powell, Thomas, and Betty Powell. *The Avant Gardener*. Box 489, New York, New York 10028. The best newsletter there is!

68. Rae, Norman. *The Garden That Cares for Itself.* San Francisco, California: Ortho Books, 1990.
69. Smith, Mary Riley, *The Front Garden.* Boston, Massachusetts: Houghton Mifflin Co., 1991.

BOOKS ON ERGONOMICS AND HORTICULTURAL THERAPY

The literature on horticultural therapy is extensive, and if this is your interest you should consult the People-Plant Council (23) for a complete bibliography on the subject. We are listing some books that we feel will be useful to the home owner and the professional landscape designer.

70. Beems, Julia. *Adaptive Garden Equipment: Raised Bed Gardening.* Englewood, Colorado: Craig Hospital, 1986. Excellent source list for information and products.
71. Bricklin, Mark, Mark Golin, Deborah Grandinetti, and Alex Liberman. *Positive Living and Health.* Emmaus, Pennsylvania: Rodale Press, 1990.
72. Cloet, Audrey, and C. Underhill. *Gardening Is for Everyone.* London, England: Souvenir Press, n.d.
73. Cronkite, David, and Karin Perry. *The Green Medicine Tree.* St. Catharines, Ontario: Manning Press, 1990.
74. Downer, John. *Supersense.* London, England: BBC Enterprises Ltd., 1988.
75. Droscher, Vitus B. *The Magic of the Senses.* New York, New York: Harper and Row, 1971.

76. Editors of Prevention Magazine. *Life Span Plus.* Emmaus, Pennsylvania: Rodale Press, 1990.

77. Ettlinger, Steve. *The Complete Illustrated Guide to Everything Sold in Garden Centers.* New York, New York: Macmillan Publishing Co., 1990.

78. Falk, Ursula A. *On Our Own: Independent Living for Older Persons.* Buffalo, New York: Prometheus Books, 1989.

79. Gore, Dr. Irene. *Add Years to Your Life and Life to Your Years.* Briarcliff Manor, New York: Stein and Day, 1974.

80. Grandjean, E. *Fitting the Task to the Man: An Ergonomic Approach.* London, England: Taylor and Francis, 1985.

81. Grodon, Michael, M.D. *A Medical Guide for Seniors.* Radnor, Pennsylvania: Chilton Book Co., 1981.

82. *Growth Point.* Journal of Horticultural Therapy. Goulds Ground, Vallis Way, Frome, Somerset, England.

83. Houston, Jean. *The Possible Human.* New York, New York: St. Martin's Press, 1982.

84. Montagu, Ashley. *Growing Young.* New York, New York: McGraw-Hill Ltd., 1981. Exploring neoteny to help you stay young all your life.

85. Moore, Bibby. *Growing with Gardening.* Chapel Hill, North Carolina: University of North Carolina Press, 1989.

86. Please, Peter. *Able to Garden,* London, England: BT Batsford. For disabled and elderly English gardeners.

87. Presman, Curtis. *How a Man Ages*. New York, New York: Ballantine/Esquire, 1984.

88. Relf, Diane. *The Role of Horticulture in Human Well-Being and Social Development*. Portland, Oregon: Timber Press, 1992. A comprehensive book with six associate editors to give a multi-discipline overview of all aspects of people-plant relationships, based on a 1990 national symposium.

89. ————. *Gardening in Raised Beds and Containers*. Blacksburg, Virginia: Virginia Polytechnic Institute and State University, 1989.

90. Restuccio, Jeffrey P. *Fitness the Dynamic Gardening Way*. Cordova, Tennessee: Balance of Nature Publishing Co., 1992.

91. St. Barbe-Baker, Richard. *My Life, My Trees*. Lorian Association, 568 Grand Canyon Drive, Madison, Wisconsin 53719.

92. Soyka, Fred, and Alan Edmonds. *The Ion Effect*. Toronto, Ontario: Lester and Orpen Ltd., 1977.

93. Stout, Ruth. *How to Have a Green Thumb Without an Aching Back*. New York, New York: Simon & Schuster, 1956; reprinted 1990. An early look at the value of mulching.

94. Tannenhaus, Norra. *Relief from Carpal Tunnel Syndrome and Other Repetitive Motion Disorders*. New York, New York: Dell Publishing Co., 1991.

MAGAZINES
New Publications

A recently founded organization called Garden Literature Press publishes *Garden Literature*, a quarterly index of articles of interest to hortiscape professionals and home owners, taken from over 150 magazines, journals, newsletters, and book reviews. If you'd like to get in touch with this press, its address is 398 Columbus Avenue, Suite 181, Boston, Massachusetts 02116-6008, Tel.: 617-424-1784; Fax: 617-424-1712.

If you are a collector of garden information, a librarian, or a gardener active in a garden club, you might wish to subscribe to *Garden Literature*. It will keep you fully informed of all the sources of up-to-date horticultural information. Its list now includes over 150 of the best North American magazines, and we are sure they will add more.

Better Homes and Gardens recently began publishing a line called Special Interest Publications. We have examined three — *Garden, Deck and Landscape Planner; Garden Products and Planning Guide;* and *Garden Ideas and Outdoor Living* — and found them to be an excellent way of catching up with what's new in landscaping and gardening.

Country Gardens is a publication for the outdoor gardener, covering all types of outdoor gardens and their care. The Garden Shop section lets you know what's new for your garden (Meredith Corporation, 1716 Locust Street, Des Moines, Iowa 50309).

Green Prints is the first garden magazine devoted to the human side of gardening, without the all-too-often-printed advice about how to plant petunias. You will find it inspiring and refreshing! Pat and Becky Stone came from the staff of *Mother Earth News* and now are celebrating, as they say on the cover of the first issue, by "Chasing the Soul of Gardening." *Green Prints*, Box 1355, Fairview, North Carolina 28730.

House Plant is a new magazine with a focus on information for indoor gardeners. The editor, Larry Hodgson, at one time had 600 varieties of houseplants in his city apartment, so he knows what he's writing about. Would you like to know what vitamins to feed your plants, or would you like to find out about yellow, orange, or red African violets? *House Plant* will tell you! We suggest you give it a try! *House Plant*, Inc. Box 271-2, Elkins, West Virginia 26241-9742.

Old Favorites
Here are some of the magazines that we use regularly:

American Nurseryman is the standard for trees and nursery stock for landscaping. American Nurseryman Publishing, 111 North Canal Street, Chicago, Illinois 60606-7203.
Canadian Gardening is an excellent source for the cold-climate gardener. Camar Publications Ltd., 130 Spy Court, Markham, Ontario L3R 5H6.
Country Life. If you live in the country and garden

(or aspire to both) you'll enjoy this magazine. Tele-media Communications Inc., Ferry Road, Charlotte, Vermont 05445.

Flora. One of the best of the European garden magazines. *Flora,* Vorzugs-Service, Postfach 11 16 29, 2000 Hamburg 11. Published in German.

Flower and Garden. Broad coverage, especially for the southern states. KC Publishing, 4251 Pennsylvania Avenue, Kansas City, Missouri 64111.

Garden Design. World coverage for both amateur and professional, with a dandy book section. Evergreen Publishing, 4401 Connecticut Avenue, Suite 500, Washington, D.C. 20008-2302.

Garden West. Just what the name implies, garden coverage from the Prairies to the West Coast in Canada. Cornwall Publishing Company Ltd., 4962 Granville Street, Vancouver, British Columbia V6M 3B2.

Horticulture. Always informative, entertaining garden reading. Horticulture Limited Partnership, 20 Park Plaza, Suite 1220, Boston, Massachusetts 02116.

Landscape Architecture. Journal of the American Society of Landscape Architects, 4401 Connecticut Avenue, Washington, D.C. 20008.

Landscape Architectural Review. This is the journal of the Canadian Society of Landscape Architects. Strachan-Steven Inc., 1250 Reid Street, Unit 8a, Richmond Hill, Ontario L4B 1G3.

Mother Earth News. The original country magazine, with a lot of good information on gardening. Sussex Publishing, Inc., 24 East 233rd, New York, New York 10010.

National Gardening. One of the best sources for information on food growing. National Gardening, 180 Flynn Avenue, Burlington, Vermont 05401.

Organic Gardening. Still one of the most popular, backed by the Rodale Research Farm. Rodale Press, 33 East Minor St., Emmaus, Pennsylvania 18098. The emphasis is on chemical-free growing.

Sunset. Covers 13 western states and offers a wealth of garden information. Lane Publishing Co., 80 Willow Road, Menlo Park, California 94025-3691.

TLC . . . for plants. Reflects a new attitude toward the winter garden. Broad coverage of indoor and outdoor landscaping and gardening, as well as horticultural therapy. Uses some of Canada's best garden writers. Gardenvale Publishing Co. Ltd., 1 Pacific, Ste Anne de Bellevue, Quebec H9X 1C5.

Wildflower. Comprehensive world coverage of native flora with a good reference book list. Canadian Wildflower Society, 90 Wolfrey Avenue, Toronto, Ontario M4K 1KS.

INDEX